DAVENPORT'S TEXAS WILLS AND ESTATE PLANNING LEGAL FORMS

3rd Edition : 2015
Published by Davenport Press

by Manfred Sternberg

Attorney-at-Law
4550 Post Oak Pl. Dr., Suite 119, Houston, TX 77027

www.manfredlaw.com

Phone: 713-622-4300

Email us at
manfred@manfredlaw.com

ALSO PUBLISHED BY DAVENPORT PRESS

Davenport's Florida Wills And Estate Planning Legal Forms

Davenport's Georgia Wills And Estate Planning Legal Forms

Davenport's Illinois Wills And Estate Planning Legal Forms

Davenport's Indiana Wills And Estate Planning Legal Forms

Davenport's Louisiana Wills And Estate Planning Legal Forms

Davenport's Maryland Wills And Estate Planning Legal Forms

Davenport's Massachusetts Wills And Estate Planning Legal Forms

Davenport's Michigan Wills And Estate Planning Legal Forms

Davenport's Minnesota Wills And Estate Planning Legal Forms

Davenport's Missouri Wills And Estate Planning Legal Forms

Davenport's Nebraska Wills And Estate Planning Legal Forms

Davenport's New Jersey Wills And Estate Planning Legal Forms

Davenport's New York Wills And Estate Planning Legal Forms

Davenport's North Carolina Wills And Estate Planning Legal Forms

Davenport's Ohio Wills And Estate Planning Legal Forms

Davenport's Pennsylvania Will And Estate Planning Legal Forms

Davenport's Tennessee Wills And Estate Planning Legal Forms

Davenport's Wyoming Wills And Estate Planning Legal Forms

Booklet Series

Davenport's California Will And Estate Planning Legal Forms Booklet

Davenport's Maine Will And Estate Planning Legal Forms Booklet

Davenport's Wisconsin Will And Estate Planning Legal Forms Booklet

Accounting C.P.A. Series

Davenport's Federal Estate And Gift Tax 2015 Basic Forms Review

Davenport's Spreadsheet And Print Templates For 1099-MISC 2015

Publication Description:
Title: Davenport's Texas Wills And Estate Planning Legal Forms
Edition: Third, 2015
Authors: Manfred Sternberg
Publisher: **DAVENPORT PRESS**, 54 Amelia Ave., West St. Paul, MN 55118

TABLE OF CONTENTS

INTRODUCTION BY
BOOK AUTHOR MANFRED STERNBERG

Greetings to all readers from this book's author. I am Texas lawyer Manfred Sternberg, and I have over 30 years of experience working with Texas law and helping people.

This book is especially written for people living in Texas. This book covers Wills and Estate planning legal documents which deal with how a person can do documents to control on illness, death, or absence their health care, end-of-life issues, property and money, children, funeral and burial, and more. This book provides legal forms which, if done right, are valid legal documents. This book quickly explains legal basics that should educate and remove some worries of people.

I know some people want to try creating their own legal documents to save money and hassle. However, many people after reading this book may want to use a lawyer for help. A lawyer can be very helpful by providing witnesses and a notary for a signing, making sure forms are done right, and asking questions and suggesting other options if facts warrant them. As wealth or age or any complications increase, people are more likely to need a lawyer.

MANFRED STERNBERG, Attorney-at-Law
MANFRED STERNBERG & ASSOCIATES PC
4550 Post Oak Pl. Dr., Suite 119, Houston, TX 77027
713-622-4300   manfred@manfredlaw.com

CHAPTER 1
GUIDE TO BOOK AND FORMS

THIS BOOK HAS 11 FORMS BUT MOST PEOPLE ONLY USE A FEW FORMS

This book provides and explains 11 legal forms that can make binding legal documents if completed, but most people only use a few of these forms. The legal forms in this book are:

1. **Last Will And Testament (With Guardians)** (lets a person write gifts of property and money to occur on death, pick guardians for children under 18 as well as guardian of property and money of a minor, allow less costly legal options to be used, pick an executor to handle matters, and more);

2. **Last Will And Testament (No Guardians)** (this is a Will with no "Guardians" paragraph as it is meant for people without minor children under 18 and does not give things to any minors);

3. **Self-Proving Affidavit** (this form is often done with a Will to help with the work after death of proving that a Will was signed correctly, and makes a Will more likely to be followed);

4. **Tangible Personal Property List** (A simple list that can be made to gift after death tangible personal property, like clothing or jewelry or furniture, which list is not legally binding but often is voluntarily followed by family and others);

5. **Codicil** (this can make changes to an existing Will, but most people just do a new Will);

6. **Medical Power Of Attorney** (lets health care instructions be given and person be named to control health care in case one cannot later control own health care);

7. **Directive To Physicians And Family Or Surrogates (Living Will)** (lets a person order that certain health care should stop if they are ever in a terminal condition or near death);

8. **Do-Not-Resuscitate** (this form can be requested from a doctor when in poor health to instruct paramedics and others to not try restarting the heart, breathing, or other major actions);

9. **Statutory Durable Power of Attorney** (allows power over one's money, property, and more be shared with a very trusted person, often done so they can help, do or manage things);

10. **Authorization Agreement For Nonparent Relative (Over Child)** (allows power over a child, including health care and education, be shared with any relative often in case parents are away);

11. **Appointment Of Agent To Control Disposition Of Remains** (lets a person give instructions and pick a person to control their body after death, and related matters of funeral, cremation, and burial rather than have closest family member control this or not be required to follow instructions).

THIS BOOK COVERS WILLS, ESTATE PLANNING LAW, AND FORMS

This book covers Texas Wills and Estate planning legal documents, which deal with what a person can do now to control upon their illness, death, or absence, many issues like health care, end of life issues, transfer of property and money, access to records, children, funeral and burial, and more. This book provides, in one convenient place, a quick review of some law and many ready to use legal forms to make binding legal documents. To reduce confusion and skimming, this book is short with accessible legal forms. People who later want more information can easily get more from other sources. Texas law usually applies if people live here more than temporarily.

BOOK AND FORMS SHOULD BE SUFFICIENT IN A TYPICAL SITUATION

Wills and Estate Planning forms do basic things that many people can do for themselves. Some forms also involve basic financial and family issues that may be relevant in certain situations. This book and the forms included should be sufficient for people with typical and usual situations and wishes, but only the main issues are discussed; special issues and legal complications are not covered. This book discusses many legal areas to explain basic things. Many forms in these legal areas are fairly standard, and half this book's forms are not created by a lawyer but are standard published forms by the state legislature (with instructions or written to be self-explanatory), by a state agency, or done with basic words to match a clear state law.

PEOPLE WITH UNUSUAL SITUATIONS OR WISHES MAY NEED A LAWYER

Some people may need a lawyer for Wills and Estate planning documents, especially those with unusual wishes or situations. These situations include: 1) wealth over $5 million, 2) complex family situations, 3) unusual wishes for gifts, or 4) big family medical concerns (like persons with long-term care or special needs). Using a lawyer usually can take a few visits, cost over $1,000, and results will vary. Some forms are usually redone every 5 years or so raising costs of a lawyer about ten-fold over a lifetime. Oftentimes in life people must weigh likely costs and benefits and decide whether to pay a lawyer. But as some people say, sometimes the cheapest lawyer is the most expensive, and sometimes the most expensive lawyer is the cheapest, so it is not always wise to go with the cheapest legal option. So, people must consider many things and decide whether to use a lawyer for a Will and Estate planning legal documents. Often Will and Estate planning documents are not vital and just save minor costs and work, or avoid problems using basic words a standard form has, and are not ever used or not used for decades. But sometimes such documents are vital or must deal with complicated situations calling for a lawyer despite the higher cost.

This book is not a substitute for legal advice and no lawyer-client relationship is created by this book or its forms.

SOME DOCUMENTS NOT IN THIS BOOK ARE NOT USED OFTEN

Some other legal documents aren't used frequently and are not covered in this book.

Property and debt lists are informally written each year by some people to help after their death.

"Revocable Living Trust" papers may be suggested to transfer, item by item, most of a person's things to a trust for years, mainly to have things transfer faster after death and avoid small costs and maybe a probate process. But, this is rare and can make living and paperwork difficult for years.

"Childrens Trust" papers to have a trust manage property and money of anyone under 18 getting anything in a Will or other way. A Will already lets a person name a "guardian of the estate" to manage and spend a minor's things for them until they become adults, and trusts mainly are done just to avoid small costs of a yearly court review of guardians.

"Standby Guardian" forms can be done to try to have power over children quickly go to someone if a parent dies or is incapacitated by illness, but forms alone cannot do this and a court hearing must be held, and a Will already can name guardians who a court usually confirms if needed in a few days.

"Organ Donation" forms usually are done in other forms like for a drivers license, state ID, or some of the health care forms covered in this book. If wanted, a person can sign up directly at donatelifetexas.org . A person's family can later consent to organ donation if they did not forbid it.

People in a separate form can name guardians for minor children but a Will already does this.

People who want more control or protection of money, property, family, and other things may want to use a lawyer for a kind of trust or other documents. Often a lawyer can help explain options.

DOWNLOAD OR PHOTOCOPY FORMS AND RARELY CHANGE THEM

To get forms, people can 1) download forms free as this book's Appendix A explains, or 2) photocopy pages from this book. Book pages that are forms do not have bottom page numbers. When filling out forms people can use a computer or handwrite to add words but should be sure to handwrite signatures and nearby dates in permanent ink. If you choose to handwrite, write clearly and legibly so that others can easily interpret and read your handwriting. Most forms show with blank spaces and underlining where to add words and signatures (like, "I name _____ as Agent"). This book shows some ways to change words or add language in forms, but this can have risks..

MANY PEOPLE SKIP SOME OF THIS BOOK AND SKIP USING MOST FORMS

This book goes into many legal details and legal forms that may not interest most people. Skipping some of this book and heading straight to a form is not recommended, but it probably won't harm people with usual situations or wishes. Forgoing using some of this book's forms is recommended, and most people only use 3 to 5 forms. For example, many only do a Will like Form 1, a Self-Proving Affidavit like Form 3, and a Medical Power of Attorney like Form 6.

CHAPTER 2
BASIC PROBATE LAW AND PROPERTY LAW
SOME IDEAS AND WORDS ARE BASIC TO WILLS AND ESTATE PLANNING

Some ideas and words are basic to Wills and Estate Planning law and forms.

■ <u>A person who has died is called a "decedent" or "deceased".</u>

■ A "Will" is a document made by a person to control some issues after their death. A Will is often called a "Last Will and Testament" and anyone doing a Will is called "Testator".

■ "Property" is anything of value and is: 1) "real property" which is land, buildings, and fixtures attached to land or buildings, or 2) "personal property" which is anything else like money, accounts, investments, jewelry, clothing, furniture, appliances, equipment, vehicles, etc.
The term "property" includes money in any form, like cash on hand or in accounts or other places.

■ A "beneficiary" is a person getting things without fully paying, like from a gift in a Will.

■ "Heir" is a person who gets something on a death due to a Will or state law (they "inherit").

■ "Probate" is an optional legal process to help after a person's death. It can help transfer property, pick guardians, show people things were done fairly, and handle owed creditors. Texas probate, unlike some states, is fairly cheap, skips most court hearings, and has simple options.

■ An "Executor" (also called a "Personal Representative") is the person in charge of any probate process and other things after a death, and often is a spouse, adult child, or friend.

■ "Notary" (also called a "notary public") is a person approved by the state to make signing of certain documents more trustworthy and official. They can be found at banks, insurance agents, courts, some copy places, or, most conveniently, can be hired from the Internet or phonebook.

■ The word "respectively" means "in the same order just said or listed" and often is used where people sign.

■ Texas laws are called "sections" or "statutes" and are mostly organized in about 27 "Codes" like the "Education Code" or "Health and Safety Code". In 2013 the "Probate Code" was renamed the "Estates Code". The symbol "§" means section or statute, and "annotated" means the law is in a book with legal notes that help interpret the law. Various court rules may also apply. Federal law is found in the U.S. Code.

■ A form put in law by state legislators to help people (or as a sample) is a "statutory form".

■ Wills and similar issues may involve the county "Probate Court" which often has forms to use.

"ESTATE" MEANS PROPERTY LEFT FROM A DECEDENT OR MANAGING BODY

Property of a decedent that on death did not transfer automatically to other owners is called the "estate" of a decedent, or the "probate estate". Also, after a death there may be an "estate" body run by the person who is executor to do things and temporarily hold property, and a decedent's accounts and other property might be renamed for a few months like "Estate of [decedent]".

"NON-PROBATE PROPERTY" TRANSFERS AS ARRANGED NOT BY WILL

Property that for some reason automatically transfers on death to other owners is "non-probate property", and such property transfers as arranged even if a Will names the property. Examples are, a) "beneficiary" forms that name someone to get accounts or other things, b) transfer-on-death or pay-on-death accounts naming someone are used, c) property is held by several people as "joint tenants" with rights of survivorship, d) an "enhanced life estate deed" is filed (this can be reversed during life), and e) insurance names a person as beneficiary. Arranging non-probate transfers is called "avoiding probate" if it is done for most things. However, this is rare as it can make living and paperwork difficult for years. Basically, when doing a Will people should consider non-probate transfers that may occur and plan accordingly.

OWNERSHIP OF PROPERTY DETERMINES WHAT CAN BE GIFTED

A person can only gift by Will or other way property and money they own.

Very basically, in Texas a person usually owns all they earn. A person also owns things or parts of things that their resources contribute funds to get or improve.

A person owns inheritances and gifts made just to them, even if they are married.

People can change owners in many ways, like by agreement (a verbal agreement is fine in some cases), a gift (a verbal gift is fine in some cases or often a name is just added), or not keeping track of things (often the law gives rights if money or property can't be clearly traced to certain people).

For property with a real title (real estate or vehicles) or where people list owners (like accounts) the named persons are owners unless people can prove a mistake, an agreement to share or return, or they worked or gave resources to get or improve things, not as a gift, and should be an owner.

There are many ways several people can own and have rights in the same property.

Naming property in a Will does not limit a person's power to make gifts, sell, or otherwise transfer property. Family often say a decedent in life gave them some things that are named in a Will.

But Texas is a "community property" state where a spouse, if there is one, often owns half a spouse's income and gains, and this is explained a bit later in this book.

Basically, people doing a Will should review paperwork and ask questions to see what they own and can gift in a Will or other ways.

SPOUSES OFTEN OWN PROPERTY AS "COMMUNITY PROPERTY" OWNED 50/50

In Texas, a married person's property and money is often "community property" and is owned by both spouses, each spouse with roughly a 50% share. This is different from "separate property" that a person owns all of, and the spouse has no legal interest. This occurs because Texas is a "community property" state with laws based on Spanish law and ideas of partnership and fairness. Basically, the usual rule of community property is gains during marriage are shared 50/50. The law and a judge presumes a living or recently dead married person's property, and money is community property unless evidence shows an exception. These separate property exceptions include:

1) property or money can be traced to times before marriage or when in a non-community state,

2) property or money was a gift or inheritance made to a particular spouse, or

3) property was bought or improved using separate property (so tracing of funds can be vital).

Based on these principles, money is usually gained from a married person's job and is community property owned by both spouses, no matter where the money is held. The same 50/50 share goes for things like cars, investments, and real property gained during marriage. Property bought with debt like a loan, credit card, or mortgage is usually community property unless a creditor agreed to never make claims on a spouse. Even income from separate property like dividends or interest, earned during marriage is community property. However, increases in value of separate property is separate property (unless a spouse's labor or community property caused the increase like repairs or improvements). Money from a spouse to the other spouse's separate property like repairs, improvements, or mortgage payments may create a right to "reimbursement" of money paid or right to own part of property. Although rare, a lawyer's pre or post-nuptial agreement can limit rights.

REAL PROPERTY IS USUALLY OWNED WHICH CAN LIMIT GIFTS

Real property (land, buildings, and fixtures tied to the land) is usually owned according to the title papers, which can limit power to sell or gift, like:

a) normal or "separate" ownership usually occurs if just 1 person is listed on title, then the owner usually has power to sell or gift during life and to gift by Will;

b) "tenants in common" may occur if several people are listed on title, then an owner has a percent share (like 50%) they can sell or gift in life or also gift by Will (this is a fairly common);

c) "joint tenant with right of survivorship" occurs if several are named on title and this is said, then an owner has a percent share (like 50%) they can sell or gift during life but can't gift by Will since on death it goes to other named owners (this is how married couples often own their house);

d) a "life estate" occurs if title papers use these words, then a person uses a property for their life but can't sell or gift it in life or gift by Will because on death things go to others named on the title;

e) "trust property" occurs when paperwork creates a trust and people, item by item, created paperwork to transfer property into the trust, then only a "trustee" in charge can sell or gift trust property in ways the trust allows, and Wills can't usually can't affect or gift trust property.

Texas does not use "tenants by the entirety" type of ownership for married people or others. Things that are not real property, like accounts, can be owned in these complex ways.

IF NO WILL THEN "INTESTATE" LAW CONTROLS PROPERTY

"Intestate" means to die with no Will. <u>Only if there is no Will then this law directs estate property</u> (property that didn't transfer automatically on death) based on what family members are left):

a) If a person left no spouse but left descendants (children, grandchildren), descendants get all;

b) If a person left no spouse and no descendants, then each surviving parent gets 50% of property and any remainder goes to brothers and sisters or their descendants (if no brothers or sisters or their descendants survive then any parent takes all);

c) If a person left no spouse, descendants, parents, or brothers or sisters or their descendants, then more distant family get property;

d) If a person leaves a spouse and also descendants who are all related to the spouse, a spouse gets a) 1/3 decedent's separate "personal property" (i.e., not real estate), b) for spouse's life use of 1/3 decedent's separate real estate, and c) all community property, and descendants get rest;

e) If a person leaves a spouse and some descendants not related to the spouse, a spouse gets a) 1/3 decedent's separate property, b) for spouse's life use of 1/3 decedent's separate real estate, and c) 1/2 community property (i.e., the 1/2 the spouse owned), and descendants get the rest; and

f) If a person leaves a spouse but no descendants, a spouse gets a) all decedent's separate personal property, b) all community property, and c) 1/2 decedent's separate real estate (decedent's parents and brothers or sisters or their descendants get the other 1/2 of decedent's separate real estate, but if none survive then a spouse gets this).

In these laws, descendants take for a dead ancestor (like grandchildren take for a dead parent).

For these laws adopted children count as a child of a person, but not foster or step-children.

This intestate distribution of property and money usually does not occur if there is a Will.

USUALLY NO FEDERAL OR TEXAS TAX IS OWED ON A DEATH

Usually little tax is owed due to a death, despite what many people think.

First, the Federal Estate And Gift Tax taxes transfers made in life or that occur on death and some insurance, but it only starts if a tax credit is used up covering $5,430,000 in transfers after 2014.

Second, another state's estate or inheritance tax can be owed for things located there or going to persons there, but just 15 states have such taxes, and they usually start at over $2,000,000.

Third, Texas has no estate, inheritance, or similar taxes that are related to a person dying.

PROPERTY IS FIRST USED TO PAY OFF DEBTS OF CREDITORS BEFORE WILL

Usually creditors owed by a decedent must be paid before gifts made by Will or other transfers occur. Paying creditors uses some of a decedent's property and money, so can interfere with Will gifts. Texas law, in some cases, does not require ordinary creditors be told about a death, so some people may want to consider looking into not paying some creditors after a death. To pay debts a decedent's property and money is used in a certain order:

1) first used is property passing by Will residue clause (which is property no other Will part used),

2) next used to pay debts are things in Will "general gifts" (like plain gifts of money), and

3) last used to pay debts is property in Will specific gifts (where property is specifically described).

To pay creditors non-probate transfers can be undone if all other property has been used up. Usually family need not pay a debt unless they co-signed or guaranteed.

For married persons some rules about debts apply:

a) community property, which both spouses had some ownership of, may have to be used to pay a decedent's debts made or increased during marriage, but a spouse's separate property and "special community property" controlled by them usually are protected from creditors;

b) a decedent's separate property should be used first before community property to pay debts related to only 1 spouse like funeral costs; and

c) a spouse's "duty of support" can make paying for medical care and housing unavoidable.

SECURED DEBTS LIKE MORTGAGES AND CAR LIENS NOT USUALLY PAID

In Texas, after a death, usually secured debts like mortgages or car liens are not paid off and instead remain on property. Whoever gets property by Will or other way from a decedent usually must keep paying such debts to keep the property. But a Will can say secured debts should be paid off, like "Before gifts in this Will occur all debts should be paid on my '89 Buick and my property at 9 Rex Rd., Ivy, TX". A simpler option in a Will is to give some money to help pay secured debts.

FAMILY GET "ALLOWANCE" AND "EXEMPT PROPERTY" BEFORE CREDITORS

Texas law does give a spouse, or children under 18, or dependent children some rights to property before creditors are paid and before a Will is carried out. Family often don't bother using rights if a Will gives them most things, but rights can greatly help family get things if decedent owed creditors a lot. Costs for a funeral and final illness up to $15,000 usually must be paid before family rights.

"Family Allowance" rights give family the right to money for 1 year to help with living costs from a decedent's estate property. The amount awarded, raised using decedent's accounts and selling property, is what is needed after considering a surviving spouse's "separate property" a spouse has and could use. If possible, a family allowance is raised without selling property in specific gifts in the Will and is usually paid from both decedent's separate and community property.

"Exempt Property" rights give family the right to pick $60,000 of decedent's tangible personal property (like furniture, clothes, tools, a vehicle for every family member and up to $15,000 jewelry). During any probate process, family can use this property, and then if the estate is insolvent without enough to pay debts family keeps this property, or if the estate is not insolvent, this property passes as a Will or state law says. A secured debt on such property does remain like a car lien. Also, if (as is common) a decedent does not have enough exempt property an "allowance in lieu of exempt property" can be paid to family of $30,000 (or whatever amount is needed to reach $30,000).

Also, state and federal law exempts from creditor claims most wages not yet paid, retirement accounts, pensions, college savings plans, and most insurance.

BEFORE CREDITORS "HOMESTEAD" (OR $45,000 CREDIT) GOES TO FAMILY

More than most states Texas law protect the "homestead", which is a person's house and 10 urban acres of residential property or 200 rural acres (or 100 acres if unmarried). Out buildings and mixed business use property, usually count too. Which person actually owns a homestead depends on who provided the funds to buy, improve, or pay down the debt on the homestead, and often 2 spouses each own a 50% "community interest". It is possible, however, that it was bought before marriage or somehow did not use major community property funds, so it is owned "separate property" of one spouse.

The first Texas right to protect a homestead is the "Occupancy" right of a spouse for life, or minor children until age 18 to live in decedent's homestead. A person can still gift ownership of a homestead they own or 50% own as community property, but a spouse or children for years have this right to occupy (due to this, many people, to avoid problems, gift a homestead to a spouse or minor child or add them to the deed). During occupancy mortgages and taxes must be paid.

The second Texas right to protect a homestead is the "Homestead Exemption" that says, except for mortgages and taxes, most creditors of decedent have no claim on decedent's homestead if decedent at death had a spouse or minor child (or adult child, too, if they are living in the homestead). Importantly, if a decedent did not own a homestead (i.e., the family are renters) an "allowance in lieu of homestead" of $45,000 can be paid from a decedent's things before creditors are paid, which goes to a decedent's spouse, minor child, or dependent incapacitated child. Homestead rights are in addition to the "family allowance" and "exempt property" rights covered in this book earlier.

SPOUSE USUALLY FOLLOWS WILL EVEN IF IT GIFTS SOME OF THEIR THINGS

A surviving spouse must decide if to follow a Will and get the gifts in a Will, at the cost of accepting other parts of a Will. This is often called the "spousal election" or "widow's election". This often involves a surviving spouse accepting a Will giving away property the spouse owns or partly owns (like community property owned 50%), which is accepted because a Will gives the spouse other property and money. For example, a spouse may elect to follow a Will which gifts and gains them 100% of the family house and 80% of the couple's other property but, less favorably, gives to children or friends 20% of the couple's property like some accounts or household items. A spouse who decides to "elect against a Will" keeps legal ownership of their property (like their 50% interest in all community property) but cannot get anything by the Will (so Will gifts to a spouse electing against a Will are ignored). <u>Basically, most people give a spouse enough in a Will so they'll want to follow a Will, even if it gifts away property fully or partly owned by the spouse.</u>

DO NEW WILL IF DIVORCE, MARRY, HAVE NEW CHILD, OR MOVE STATES

Divorcing, marrying, having a new child, or moving to a new state after writing a Will can have legal effects. If any of these occur people probably should do a new Will and review other papers.

SIMPLER PROBATE PROCESS CAN BE USED IN MANY PROBATE CASES

If full probate is done, it usually takes over 1 year and moderate cost, so other options exist.

"Independent Administration" lets some normal probate steps be skipped and involves less paperwork and court hearings, and most Wills authorize this including the Wills in this book.

"Small Estate Affidavits" can be filled out and given to banks, stock brokers, and most others to get property if there is no Will, the estate appears solvent, and there is under $50,000 in a probate estate (counting decedent's separate property and half of community property but excluding a homestead and exempt property). A homestead but not other real estate can be transferred this way.

"Small Estate Procedure" with less paperwork and usually taking under a month is available if the probate estate is not enough to pay a "family allowance" and certain creditors.

"Collection Of Final Paycheck" can be done just by a spouse asking an employer in most cases.

"Motor Vehicle Title Transfer" to get a new certificate of title may be done by filing an "affidavit of heirship" with a county tax assessor's officer.

Other Texas options are Muniment of Title, Order of No Administration, Unqualified Community Administration, Nonstatutory Affidavit of Heirship, and an Heirship Proceeding.

Importantly, "Ancillary Probate" is a costly court proceeding in another state done for property located there (often real estate) unless certain legal exceptions apply. Helpfully, Ancillary Probate in another state often can be avoided by holding property jointly with another person so it transfers to them on death, so this is often recommended.

CHAPTER 3
WILL BASICS

"WILL" IS DOCUMENT OFTEN DONE TO CONTROL ISSUES AFTER DEATH

A "Will" is a legal document that can be done by any person of sound mind, at least age 18 to control many issues that may arise after their death. Issues can include who gets money and property, who will manage things as executor, if faster legal procedures can be used, and who will be guardians, if needed, of children under 18 and any minor's property. Not doing a Will can cause confusion, more costs, hearings, delay, and family fights. A Will is often called a "Last Will and Testament" and the person making a Will is called the "Testator". Texas law applies to a Will if a person resides in or plans to return to Texas, even if the date is uncertain (so often includes college students or military personnel living outside of Texas). A Will can be enforced in the 4 years after a death, or if certain exceptions apply. In any legal process, most persons get a copy of a Will.

WILL SHOULD BE SIGNED WITH 2 DISINTERESTED WITNESSES

To be valid, most Texas Wills are signed by the person doing the Will before 2 witnesses who then also sign. Normally, witnesses only read or have read to them the paragraph they are signing. Witnesses must be at least age 14, and if possible using witnesses young enough to be available later if needed is best. The Will maker and the 2 witnesses should see each others' hands as they hold a permanent ink pen or marker and sign. No particular words need to be said, but the Will maker often says, "This is the Will I want, and want you two persons to witness". Witnesses should be "disinterested witnesses" that are not getting gifts in the Will, since acting as witness usually undoes any Will gifts to them (except if under "intestate law" they as close family would get things if there were no Will). Witnesses can be a spouse or other family, or the person named executor or guardian in a Will, but it is recommended that people without these ties are used as witnesses.

SELF-PROVING AFFIDAVIT DOCUMENT OFTEN IS DONE WITH A WILL

Often a Self-Providing Affidavit document is also done when a Will is signed, or some later time by everyone signing this document before a notary. This book's Chapter 7 explains this more, and has a form for people to do this. If this is not done, usually one witness to a Will signing must be found after a death and testify in court to show a Will was signed correctly and should be followed. In some cases, other evidence can show this. <u>Doing a Self-Providing Affidavit to support a Will is recommended and is common</u>. However, getting everyone before a notary to do a Self-Proving Affidavit can be difficult and is not legally required to do a Will. Some benefits of a lawyer are they often have a notary, can provide witnesses if needed, and they make sure a Will is signed right.

"HOLOGRAPHIC" WILL WITHOUT WITNESSES NOT RECOMMENDED

Usually Wills are signed before 2 witnesses but technically Texas law does allow a Will without witnesses if a Will is written by hand (not typed or computer printed) by the person doing the Will. A Will without witnesses is called a "Holographic Will". However, this means that later two people who know the person's writing would have to be found and testify convincingly in court. A Will done without two witnesses is rare and is not recommended. Since it must be handwritten, it requires additional proof later, such Wills often leave out very helpful legal language, such Wills face more costs and delays and lawsuits, and such Will are more often not followed.

KEEP WILL IN SAFE PLACE IT WILL BE FOUND

When done, a Will should be kept in a safe place where it will be found within days of death such as a desk, filing cabinet, in a safe (if someone else has access), or a safe deposit box (legally bank employee can look inside for a Will or similar forms). Some people give a Will to a spouse or friend or tell them where to look. A Will can also be put for safekeeping at the local Probate court.

WILL CAN BE REVOKED BY NEW WILL, TEARING UP, OR MARKING

To cancel or "revoke" a Will, a person can do a new Will which says it revokes previous Wills, or they can personally do acts showing intent to revoke like tearing up, burning, or writing "canceled" on pages. Revoking a Will does not usually bring back into force earlier Wills.

IN WILL CAN NAME "EXECUTOR" TO HANDLE MATTERS AFTER DEATH

Most Wills name an "executor" to, if needed, do things after a death like manage probate, find and transfer property and money, do paperwork, and pay bills. A person named executor in a Will often is a spouse, adult child, or friend (or a lawyer or bank if they agree). The executor can live outside Texas, but they must name a local person like a friend or lawyer to accept any papers.

A person guilty of a felony or serious misconduct cannot act as executor. The person named executors can be getting Will gifts and can be named as guardian in a Will. If needed, and no Will names an executor, a judge in a costly, long hearing picks from a spouse and family who may argue about this. Naming two persons to be executor at the same time is less common due to possible legal problems and delays. Executors are paid back for any fees and costs they pay. Many Wills say an executor is to get no compensation (this book's Wills do this), but if a Will is silent an executor can request a fee of 5% of certain property sales and receipts (but not cash or money in accounts). An executor asking for pay is often skipped as this uses up estate assets and is taxable income. State law also calls an executor a "Personal Representative".

IF USED A LAWYER FOR EXECUTOR IS PAID USING ESTATE PROPERTY

If an executor finds they need help of a lawyer (a few judges require this), a lawyer is paid for using some of the decedent's money or property. A lawyer is usually paid what the executor agreed to, often either under $3,000 or $200/hour, which is low given the big amounts maybe involved.

EXECUTOR HAS POWER TO EASILY COLLECT AND TRANSFER PROPERTY

An executor, by law, has power to easily collect and transfer most property and money of a decedent. Banks, investment companies, and others will usually follow instructions of an executor. Most Wills also have a part where executors are given more powers to help them do things.

WILL CAN NAME "GUARDIAN OF THE PERSON" TO CARE FOR CHILDREN

If a parent dies with a child under 18, the other natural or adopted parent (but not a step-parent) takes over automatically unless found "unfit" by a court, which is rare. In case it is ever needed, a parent in a Will can name a "guardian of the person" to care for a child under 18, a choice which court follows unless a person clearly is not suitable. Preference of the last parent to die is given more weight. If needed and no Will names a guardian, a judge in a costly, long hearing picks from family who may argue about this. Texas law does not favor two persons both having power as guardian, unless they are a married couple, and even then it is less common. Basically, in a Will, since naming the other parent as guardian of the person is pointless (they take over unless unfit), most people name for this a healthy relative or friend. People without a child under 18 can skip or fill in a guardian clause anyway, or use a Will without this.

WILL CAN NAME "GUARDIAN OF THE ESTATE" FOR A MINOR'S PROPERTY

In a Will, a "guardian of the estate" can be named to manage property and money of those under 18, and decide how to use these to help pay for health, education and living costs until they are an adult when anything left is handed over to them. By law, persons under 18 can own but cannot control major property, and banks and others may refuse to deal with them in larger matters. Courts follow a parent's choice for guardian of the estate unless a person clearly is not suitable. If needed and no Will names a guardian of the estate, a judge in a costly, long hearing picks from a parent and family who may argue about this. Often the person who is "guardian of the person" is also named guardian of the estate, unless they are bad with money. Basically, when naming a guardian of the estate in a Will either 1) a minor will likely get things when one parent is still alive so the parent is named for this, or 2) a minor will likely get things only if all parents are dead so a friend or relative is named for this. Those without children under 18 and not giving things to minors can skip or fill in anyway a guardian clause or use a Will without this.

DUE TO COSTS AND HASSLE MANY PEOPLE AVOID GIFTING TO MINORS

A guardian of the estate does face extra work and costs to manage and spend a minor's property, and each year there is a court review looking for misuse. Due to extra work and costs, many people avoid gifting to those under 18. Some people give via family, like "I give $8 to Ann Fox in the hope she will help her son Leo Fox". However, a helpful new law, the Uniform Transfers To Minors Act, says a "custodian" process with less costs and work can manage a minor's property, and often Wills says a guardian of the estate can act like a custodian to avoid work and costs (this book's Wills do this).

WILL CAN HAVE "ALTERNATE" EXECUTOR OR GUARDIANS BUT THIS IS RARE

If a person named in a Will as executor or guardian dies or is unavailable, most people can just write a new Will or a judge will pick someone to serve if needed. To plan ahead for the rare case someone named executor or guardian dies or is unavailable, people can modify a Will to name an "alternate" person, which is done by adding after a name:

"or if they are reasonably unable to serve I nominate ___ to serve".

IN WILL CAN ASK FOR "INDEPENDENT" PROBATE AND NO "BOND"

Most Wills say informal and "Independent Administration" is wanted, which is a popular Texas probate process with less delay, paperwork, and usually one court hearing, lasting 10 minutes at most. Most Wills also have helpful language saying no "bond" or "surety" is required, which is costly insurance against bad conduct of an executor, paid for using estate funds (which should not be needed since the executor is trusted). Most Wills also say any other less costly probate options should be used if possible.

WILLS IGNORE PLURAL AND GENDER OF WORDS

Most Will forms say singular, plural, or gender meaning of words will be ignored which lets people write in blank spaces anything they want. For example, since a Will says this people can write in a blank space a woman's name or man's name, or write in one name or many names, all without worrying if it matches surrounding words. For this reason many Wills use "they" when a space might refer to just one person so seems to call for "he" or "she".

WILLS HAVE LONG "MISCELLANEOUS" SECTION TO HELP AVOID PROBLEMS

Most Wills have a long "Miscellaneous" section with many sentences of legal language that help avoid some possible legal problems and which help explain parts of the Will.

CHAPTER 4
GIFTING IN WILLS

PERSON USUALLY FREE TO GIFT BY WILL PROPERTY HOWEVER WANTED

The main use of a Will is for a person to say how they want their property to transfer on death, which is usually called gifts or gifting. In Texas, a person is largely free to gift property however they want, including not giving property to children or other family ("disinheriting" them with no legal requirement to give them anything). Texas law does give a spouse and children certain limited rights to claim property, which are discussed earlier in this book (such as rights to exempt property, allowance for year, rights to the homestead, and a spouse's 50% share of community property).

WILLS USE NORMAL WORDS TO TRANSFER MOST THINGS AFTER DEATH

A Will is the normal way a person says what happens to their property and money after their death. To do gifts in a Will often very simple words are used, like "I give ____ to ____", and the law no longer requires words like "devise", "bequeath", or "legacy". A Will gift need not be written perfectly so long as, after all evidence (including hearing from people who knew a decedent), the likely meaning of a Will gift can be seen.

IN A WILL CAN DO SPECIFIC GIFTS TO GIFT PARTICULAR PROPERTY

Most Wills, in their main area, have many "Specific Gift" sentences to let people gift particular property to persons who are named. Specific gifts can be any kind of property like clothing, jewelry, furniture, tools, cars, investments, accounts, and real estate. Specific gifts are given some preference and are carried out before most other Will gifts, and if possible the law tries to pay a decedent's debts and family rights not using things in specific gifts. Examples of specific gifts are:

"I give 1.2 carat diamond ring to Jo Dodd",

"I give UBank account ending in 8473 to Ivy Dee",

"I give all clothing to Ann Coe",

"I give 291 Lake Road, Kilby, TX, including land, buildings, and fixtures to Ann Jo Knox".

IN A WILL CAN DO GENERAL GIFTS OF MONEY AMOUNTS

Many people in a Will give "general gifts", which are any gifts that don't involve specific property. These gifts are usually money. An example of a money gift is, "I give $100 to Ed Doe". Later, an executor will have power to use money in accounts or sell property to easily carry out money gifts. Even if a Will gifts money, a person can still agree with an executor to take some property instead. Money gifts are often written with a Will's specific gifts but legally they are different. For gifts to several people, "I give $90 to Bo Lee and Jo Kim" means the same as "I give a total of $90 to Bo Lee and Jo Kim", but using the words "total" or "each" may avoid confusion.

"RESIDUE CLAUSE" IN WILL HELPFULLY GIVES ANYTHING LEFT OVER

Most Wills have a "residue clause" towards their end that gives any property and money of a person not used by other Will parts or by other means to persons named. This "catch-all" ensures everything goes to someone. Many people also use a residue clause to give most their things since this has less legal risks and avoids having to describe property. Often a Will's residue clause has:

1) a 1st space to name one or more persons to get things if they are living at the Will maker's death (many name a spouse or closest family here), and

2) a 2nd space to name people to get things if all in the 1st space don't survive (the share of anyone named in the 2nd space who don't survive usually goes to their descendants).

People should consider if debts to be paid, earlier gifts in a Will, and any non-probate transfers may leave little for a residue clause to give.

WILLS GIFTS USUALLY ARE CARRIED OUT IN A CERTAIN ORDER

When Will gifts are carried out by law they usually occur in a certain order, which is:

1) Will "specific gifts" that name particular property are done first,

2) Will "general gifts" like money amounts are done next, and then

3) a Will "residue" gift is done last (which is basically anything remaining).

Gifts of the same type usually occur in the order written in a Will. People should consider if gifts carried out earlier may leave less for later Will gifts.

WILL GIFTS NOT OF MONEY BUT OF PROPERTY ARE RISKIER

Will gifts of property not money can change and even fail for many reasons, like a) property changed in value so a recipient gets far less value, b) property is claimed by family using legal rights, c) property is sold or given away by a person before death so it is no longer available to give, or d) property has to be sold to pay a decedent's debts. For many reasons, in a Will, rather than gift property, it may be better to gift money or gift using a Will "residue" clause (which gives all remaining property to persons named).

"CONDITIONS" CAN BE PUT ON A GIFT THAT MUST BE MET

"Conditions" can be put on a gift so that if something does not occur the gift does not occur, like "I give all jewelry to Sue Lott if she loses 50 pounds" or "I give $90 to Amy Coe if she starts college". But, gift conditions, if strange or not of limited time, can lead to delay, lawsuits, and hurt feelings. Gift conditions against public policy, like if they are too restrictive, might be ignored.

17

THAT BENEFICIARY MUST "SURVIVE" TO GET GIFT IS USUAL CONDITION

Most Will gifts say "if they survive me" which means, for a gift to occur, the named beneficiary must be alive at the Will maker's death. A gift of no effect due to someone not surviving leaves the gifted property to follow later Will parts like a residue clause. To avoid legal problems, most Wills define "survive" as outliving the Will maker by 60 days. If survival is not a gift condition then who gets a gift if a beneficiary has died depends on complex state law but sometimes it is the beneficiary's children.

ALTHOUGH RARELY NEEDED "ALTERNATE BENEFICIARY" CAN BE ADDED

For the beneficiaries named to get Will gifts usually 1) they survive to get the gift, 2) they don't survive but this is seen and a Will is rewritten, or 3) they don't survive and survival was listed as a gift condition so property then goes to who a person chose in a Will's residue clause (often this is a spouse or child). If desired a person can name an "alternate beneficiary" to get a gift if the named beneficiary does not survive as required. This is done by removing from the Will gift words like "if they survive me" and adding, "but if they fail to survive me then to _____".
An example is, "I give $900 to Ed Dee but if they fail to survive me then to Jo Wu".

FAMILY CAN BE ALTERNATE BENEFICIARY USING "LINEAL DESCENDANTS"

Although rarely needed (as explained above) a person can have a beneficiary's descendants (like children or grandchildren) be alternate beneficiaries in case the person doesn't survive to get a gift. This can be done by removing "if they survive me" gift language and adding there "or their lineal descendants per stirpes". The phrase "per stirpes" in the Latin language means "by the root" and means property is split among family branches, with younger generations taking for a dead parent. A spouse is not a "descendant" so this language does not benefit anyone's spouse. An example is:

A man named Abe has two children Viv and Mort each of whom have two children. If Abe and Mort die, and Abe's Will says "to Viv and Mort or lineal descendants per stirpes" the result is Viv gets 50% and Mort's two children each get 25%.

SEVERAL PERSONS CAN GET SAME GIFT BUT GIFT IS SPLIT BY SURVIVORS

The same property or money can be gifted to several people to share, like "I give AmBank account ending in 8483 to Ed Coe and Jill Hill". Importantly, most Wills say for a gift to several persons, if any have not survived, other beneficiaries of the same gift take the non-survivor's share. So, "I give $90 to Jan, Ada, and Kay Smith if they survive me" usually means if Ada has died the other two persons get $45 each. Most Wills say a gift will be sold and money passed on if beneficiaries don't agree how to use or sell it.

BENEFICIARIES CAN GET PERCENTAGE RATHER THAN EQUAL SHARE

When several people are given the same Will gift this usually means they get an equal share, but. if wanted, a percentage can be written in to give such a share. Often a Will's "residue clause" is gifted by percentages to get the exact split wanted. Examples of Will gifts using percentages are:

"I give all tools 70% to Ed Coe and 30% to Max Dodd",

"I give 372 Lake Road, Knox, PA, 60% to Tom Dee and 40% to Ned Bund", and

"I give the residue 90% to Sue Ann Nox my wife, 6% to Max Jay Nox, and 4% to Kay Ann Hill".

WILLS NEED SUFFICIENT DESCRIPTIONS OF PERSONS LIKE A FULL NAME

The person doing a Will should usually use their full legal name in all places, including when signing. Some people add that they are known by another name, but this is not required (like, "I am also known as Big Smith" or "a/k/a Big Smith"). Those getting Will gifts must be described well enough so an executor, after listening to people who knew a decedent and looking at circumstances, can tell who likely is meant. A Will gift with a first and last name is usually enough, with any added middle name and any "Junior" helping, but often a nickname is fine, too. Family in a Will are usually called by their normal names. It may help to say how a person is known, like "from school", "my aunt", and "my New York friend". People can call up a charity to get the official name or people can just explain how the charity is known (like "the local animal shelter" or "my old church"). Wills can skip names if who is in a group is clear, like "I give $90 to each of my sister Kim's kids". Some people give a pet and money for pet care to a friend (like, "I give my cat Bo and $90 to Jo Dee") or get a lawyer's "Pet Trust". Examples of names in Wills are:

"I give $95 to Tom Smith my mechanic",

"I give my boat to Big Bjorg, Mary Smith, and Greg Paul Coe Jr.", and

"I give $800 to Bloomington Happy Meals a food charity in my county".

WILLS NEED SUFFICIENT DESCRIPTIONS OF PROPERTY GIFTED

Property in Will gifts must be described so those who knew a decedent can tell the likely meaning. This is easy as most people only own one of something to give. It is also OK to describe property by category, by standard location, or to have a long list of property in a single gift. For real property using a correct "legal description" is best (like "Lot 2, Block 4 of Polk's Subdivision, Harris County Texas") but using a street address to give real property is allowed. Examples of describing property in Will gifts are:

"I give Ubank account ending #9283 to Mary Bing",

"I give tools usually kept in my garage and my biggest gold ring to Vera Kline", and

"I give 92 Tott Avenue, Katy, Texas, including land, buildings, and fixtures, to Ann Joy Nox".

CHAPTER 5
FORM 1: LAST WILL AND TESTAMENT (WITH GUARDIANS)

FORM 1 IS A FLEXIBLE WILL WITH A GUARDIANS PARAGRAPH

Form 1 is a flexible Will that lets people write in what gifts of property and money they want to occur after their death. The Will in Form 1 also has a "Guardians" paragraph to let a person name a "guardian of the person", if ever needed, to care for a child under 18, and name a "guardian of the estate" to manage any minor's money or property if ever needed. People with no child under 18 who are not giving anything to a person under 18 when at the Guardians paragraph can skip it, fill it in anyway, or use the Will in Form 2 without this paragraph. A Will is often called a "Last Will and Testament" and the person doing a Will is called "Testator".

WILL IN FORM 1 HAS BASIC LAYOUT WITH SEVERAL PARTS TO FILL OUT

The Will in Form 1 has a basic layout with several parts for a person to fill out to use.

To start, the Will has a place for a person making the Will to put their full legal name and county.

The 1st paragraph, "Gifts", has many spaces for a person to a) make specific gifts by a person describing particular property and naming persons to get these things, and b) make money gifts by a person writing in money amounts and naming persons to get this money.

The 2nd paragraph, "Tangible Personal Property Lists", requests people follow any gifts lists people have done although usually such lists are not legally enforceable under Texas law.

The 3rd paragraph, "Residue", gives any property and money not used by other parts of the Will or in other ways, which is done by writing here the names of persons to get this.

The 4th paragraph, "Administration", has a space to write someone's name to be "executor" to if needed handle most matters after a person's death, and often named is a spouse, child, or friend.

The 5th paragraph, "Guardians", has a space to name someone "guardian of the person" to if needed care for a child under 18, and to name someone "guardian of the estate" to if needed manage property and money of any minor and spend this on them until they are 18 and get anything left.

The 6th paragraph, "Miscellaneous", just has many sentences of legal language that help avoid certain legal problems and help explain the Will.

Last is where the Will maker signs their full name and then 2 witnesses sign

As just explained, the Will parts let people gift specific property and money, say any gift lists should be followed, gift the residue, name an executor, name guardians, and have the person doing the Will and two witnesses sign the end to make it legal.

RESIDUE CLAUSE HAS 2 PLACES TO NAME PEOPLE TO GET ANYTHING LEFT

In a Will's "residue clause", anything not used by other parts of the Will or other means is gifted to the persons named in the residue clause. A residue clause is a "catch-all", making sure all property and money goes to someone. Many people use the residue clause to gift most of their things, since this has less legal risks and avoids having to describe property. The residue clause in this book's Wills is written to have:

1) a 1st space to name 1 or more persons to get the residue (but anyone named here must survive to get things or their share goes to others named here), and

2) a 2nd space to name people to get things if all in the 1st space don't survive (any named here who don't survive have their share go to descendants due to language used in the Will).

Most people name in the 1st space a spouse or closest family and in the 2nd space name their next closest family or friends. Helpful special options exist which many people can use:

a) People can in the residue clause leave the 1st space empty and only name people in the 2nd space to ensure if someone named dies their descendants get their share;

b) People can repeat names in the 2 clause spaces if there is only 1 person or group to target; and

c) People can in either of the residue clause's spaces gift using percentages.

This may seem complex, but whoever is named in the 1st used space gets things if they survive.

WILL SHOULD BE SIGNED WITH 2 DISINTERESTED WITNESSES

To be valid, most Texas Wills should be signed by the person doing the Will before 2 witnesses who then also sign. Witnesses must be at least age 14 and if possible young enough to be available later if needed. The Will maker and the two witnesses should see each others' hands as they hold a permanent ink pen or marker and sign. No particular words need to be said, but the Will maker often says a thing like, "This is the Will I want and want you two persons to witness". Before signing, most witnesses read quietly or have read to them only the paragraph they sign below.

In paragraphs that are signed, there are places to add the date of signing, and this can be done by the person signing or beforehand by anyone. Witnesses should be "disinterested witnesses", not getting gifts in the Will, since acting as witness usually undoes any Will gifts to them (except if under "intestate law" they as close family would get things if there were no Will). Witnesses can be a spouse or other family, and can be named executor or guardian in a Will, but it is a bit better if people without these connections are used as witnesses.

FORM 1:
LAST WILL AND TESTAMENT (WITH GUARDIANS)

LAST WILL AND TESTAMENT

I, _____, of _____ County, Texas, being of sound and disposing mind and memory, do hereby make, publish, and declare this as my Last Will and Testament (called here my "Will"), and hereby expressly revoke any Wills and Codicils earlier made by me.

1. GIFTS. I give the following gifts which are specific gifts except any gifts of money amounts are general gifts.

I give _____

to _____ if they survive me.

I give _____

to _____ if they survive me.

I give _____

to _____ if they survive me.

I give _____

to _____ if they survive me.

I give _____

to _____ if they survive me.

I give _____

to _____ if they survive me.

I give _____

to _____ if they survive me.

I give _____

to _____ if they survive me.

2. TANGIBLE PERSONAL PROPERTY LISTS. I may leave signed lists or other writings giving tangible personal property, and although such writings may not be legally enforceable I request but do not require people follow such writings.

3. RESIDUE. I give the rest, residue, and remainder of my estate including all property I can distribute by Will not distributed by the preceding provisions of this Will, including any real property, personal property, or other property of any kind and wherever located, whether now owned or later acquired by me (called in this Will the "residue"), to:

_____ if they survive me, but if they all do not survive me I give the just described property to

_____ or their lineal descendants per stirpes.

Part of this residue section may be left unfilled or empty, and used parts should be given effect.

4. ADMINISTRATION. I name and appoint _____

as executor of my Will and my estate.

5. GUARDIANS. If any of my children have not reached age 18 I name and appoint

_____ to be guardian over the person of such children.

I also name and appoint _____ as guardian of the estate

for such children and their estate and property, and also for any other persons under age 18 who receive or possess property and their estate and property.

6. MISCELLANEOUS. The following applies to this Will and generally.

The priority of Will gifts of the same type is based on the order they appear in a Will.

No unfilled Will part is a mistake but is intentional, including for parts about the residue.

Any executor or guardian of any type acting under this Will or otherwise shall serve without bond, surety, or other security including for performance of their duties.

Any executor shall not be paid compensation for their work or time spent as executor.

An executor shall sell a gift unless all beneficiaries getting it agree on its use or sale.

Plural, singular, or gender meanings do not limit any Will part, such as use of "they".

The words "give" and "gift" mean the same as devise, bequest, grant, legacy or similar.

The words "survive" or "surviving" in a gift or other place creates an absolute condition that must be met or a gift fails and anti-lapse laws or similar have no effect.

Any person or entity not surviving me by 60 days shall be deemed to not survive me.

Any executor is appointed and shall serve as independent executor and independent administration may be used, and I direct no action shall be had in the county court in relation to the settlement of my estate other than the probating and recording of this Will and the return of the statutory inventory, appraisement, and list of claims of my estate.

For gifts to multiple beneficiaries a non-surviving beneficiary's share goes to other beneficiaries in proportion to shares they are taking, including for the residue or if a gift requires or mentions survival, but not if an alternate beneficiary is provided in the Will.

Any executor and guardian of any type is given as much power, authority, and discretion that may be given by law, including power to (with no liability for change in value) sell, lease, assign, mortgage, invest, operate, hold, exchange and transfer any way any property including of the estate, settle claims for or against the estate or others, do any tax action or filing, and have power of sale for real property, all with no need for inventory or filing or any act of a court or others.

Any executor has power to take any action involving an ancillary estate, give different kinds, portions or undivided interests in property to beneficiaries and assign value to all things, and do any distribution or division of my estate or property in cash or in kind.

If a gift including of household items goes to several beneficiaries the executor shall have sole discretion how to divide the gift, taking into account feelings of beneficiaries and myself.

Any executor may any time and in any amount pay debts of mine or my estate they in their sole and absolute discretion finds are valid, enforceable, timely, and fair, including of a last illness, for funeral and related things, and all with no filing or act of court or others.

If any property is distributable under this Will to a minor person, I authorize my executor or other party to make distribution to a custodian for the minor under the Uniform Transfers to Minors Act of Texas or any other state, with any person named in this Will as guardian of the estate as custodian but even if they are available my executor may nominate another person.

Any successor including of an executor or guardian of any type named in this Will shall have all powers, privileges, immunities and exemptions their predecessor had.

Not giving anything or more to my children and other family is intentional and not a mistake.

The residue includes lapsed or failed gifts, insurance paid to the estate, inheritances owed testator, and property testator had power of appointment or testamentary disposition over.

TESTATOR

IN WITNESS WHEREOF, I hereunto subscribe my name and declare, publish, and acknowledge this as my Last Will and Testament as Testator all in the presence of the witnesses signing below, this __ day of _____, 20__.

_____
Testator

WITNESSES

The foregoing instrument was signed, published, and declared by the above Testator in our presence as the Last Will and Testament of such Testator, and we the undersigned Witnesses sign our names hereunto as witnesses at the request and in the presence of the such Testator and in the presence of each other, on this __ day of _____, 20__.

_____   _____
Witness   Address

_____   _____
Witness   Address

CHAPTER 6
FORM 2: LAST WILL AND TESTAMENT (NO GUARDIANS)

FORM 2 IS A WILL WITH NO GUARDIANS PARAGRAPH

Form 2 is just like the Will in Form 1 and is flexible and lets people gift their property and money most ways. Form 2 unlike Form 1l has no "Guardians" paragraph and is a Will for a person without a child under 18, and not giving anything to any minors under 18.

WILL IN FORM 2 HAS BASIC LAYOUT WITH SEVERAL PARTS TO FILL OUT

The Will in Form 2 is like the Will in Form 1 but without a "Guardians" paragraph, and it has a basic layout with several parts for a person to fill out to use.

To start, the Will has a place for a person making the Will to put their full legal name and county.

The 1st paragraph, "Gifts", has many spaces for a person to a) make specific gifts by a person describing particular property and naming persons to get these things, and b) make money gifts by a person writing in money amounts and naming persons to get this money.

The 2nd paragraph, "Tangible Personal Property Lists", requests people follow any gifts lists people have done although usually such lists are not legally enforceable under Texas law.

The 3rd paragraph, "Residue", gives any property and money not used by other parts of the Will or in other ways, which is done by writing here the names of persons to get this.

The 4th paragraph, "Administration", has a space to write someone's name to be "executor" to if needed handle most matters after a person's death, and often named is a spouse, child, or friend.

The 5th paragraph, "Miscellaneous", just has many sentences of legal language that help avoid certain legal problems and help explain the Will.

Last is where the Will maker signs their full name and then two witnesses sign.

As just explained, the Will parts let people gift specific property and money, say any gift lists should be followed, gift the residue, name an executor, name guardians, and have the person doing the Will and 2 witnesses sign the end to make it legal.

RESIDUE CLAUSE HAS 2 PLACES TO NAME PEOPLE TO GET ANYTHING LEFT

In a Will's "residue clause" anything not used by other parts of the Will or other means is gifted to the persons named in the residue clause. A residue clause is a "catch-all" making sure all property and money goes to someone. Many people use the residue clause to gift most of their things since this has less legal risks and avoids having to describe property. The residue clause in this book's Wills is written to have:

1) a 1st space to name one or more persons to get the residue (but anyone named here must survive to get things or their share goes to others named here), and

2) a 2nd space to name people to get things if all in the 1st space don't survive (any named here who don't survive have their share go to descendants due to language used in the Will).

Most people name in the 1st space a spouse or closest family and in the 2nd space name their next closest family or friends. Helpful special options exist which many people can use:

a) People can in the residue clause leave the 1st space empty and only name people in the 2nd space to ensure if someone named dies their descendants get their share;

b) People can repeat names in the 2 clause spaces if there is only 1 person or group to target; and

c) People can in either of the residue clause's spaces gift using percentages.

This may seem complex but whoever is named in the 1st used space gets things if they survive.

WILL SHOULD BE SIGNED WITH TWO DISINTERESTED WITNESSES

To be valid, most Texas Wills should be signed by the person doing the Will before two witnesses who then also sign. Witnesses must be at least age 14 and, if possible, young enough to be available later if needed. The Will maker and the two witnesses should see each others' hands as they hold a permanent ink pen or marker and sign. No particular words need to be said, but the Will maker often says a thing like, "This is the Will I want and want you two persons to witness". Before signing, most witnesses read quietly or have read to them only the paragraph they sign below. In paragraphs that are signed, there are places to add the date of signing, and this can be done by the person signing or beforehand by anyone. Witnesses should be "disinterested witnesses", not getting gifts in the Will, since acting as witness usually undoes any Will gifts to them (except if under "intestate law" they as close family would get things if there were no Will). Witnesses can be a spouse or other family, and can be named executor or guardian in a Will, but it is a bit better if people without these connections are used as witnesses.

.

FORM 2:
LAST WILL AND TESTAMENT (NO GUARDIANS)

LAST WILL AND TESTAMENT

I, _____, of _____ County, Texas, being of sound and disposing mind and memory, do hereby make, publish, and declare this as my Last Will and Testament (called here my "Will"), and hereby expressly revoke any Wills and Codicils earlier made by me.

1. GIFTS. I give the following gifts which are specific gifts except any gifts of money amounts are general gifts.

I give _____

to _____ if they survive me.

I give _____

to _____ if they survive me.

I give _____

to _____ if they survive me.

I give _____

to _____ if they survive me.

I give _____

to _____ if they survive me.

I give _____

to _____ if they survive me.

I give _____

to _____ if they survive me.

I give _____

to _____ if they survive me.

2. TANGIBLE PERSONAL PROPERTY LISTS. I may leave signed lists or other writings giving tangible personal property, and although such writings may not be legally enforceable I request but do not require people follow such writings.

3. RESIDUE. I give the rest, residue, and remainder of my estate including all property I can distribute by Will not distributed by the preceding provisions of this Will, including any real property, personal property, or other property of any kind and wherever located, whether now owned or later acquired by me (called in this Will the "residue"), to: _____ if they survive me, but if they all do not survive me I give the just described property to _____ or their lineal descendants per stirpes. Part of this residue section may be left unfilled or empty, and used parts should be given effect.

4. ADMINISTRATION. I name and appoint _____ as executor of my Will and my estate.

5. MISCELLANEOUS. The following applies to this Will and generally.

The priority of Will gifts of the same type is based on the order they appear in a Will.

No unfilled Will part is a mistake but is intentional, including for parts about the residue.

Any executor or guardian of any type acting under this Will or otherwise shall serve without bond, surety, or other security including for performance of their duties.

Any executor shall not be paid compensation for their work or time spent as executor.

An executor shall sell a gift unless all beneficiaries getting it agree on its use or sale.

Plural, singular, or gender meanings do not limit any Will part, such as use of "they".

The words "give" and "gift" mean the same as devise, bequest, grant, legacy or similar.

The words "survive" or "surviving" in a gift or other place creates an absolute condition that must be met or a gift fails and anti-lapse laws or similar have no effect.

Any person or entity not surviving me by 60 days shall be deemed to not survive me.

Any executor is appointed and shall serve as independent executor and independent administration may be used, and I direct no action shall be had in the county court in relation to the settlement of my estate other than the probating and recording of this Will and the return of the statutory inventory, appraisement, and list of claims of my estate.

For gifts to multiple beneficiaries a non-surviving beneficiary's share goes to other beneficiaries in proportion to shares they are taking, including for the residue or if a gift requires or mentions survival, but not if an alternate beneficiary is provided in the Will.

Any executor and guardian of any type is given as much power, authority, and discretion that may be given by law, including power to (with no liability for change in value) sell, lease, assign, mortgage, invest, operate, hold, exchange and transfer any way any property including of the estate, settle claims for or against the estate or others, do any tax action or filing, and have power of sale for real property, all with no need for inventory or filing or any act of a court or others.

Any executor has power to take any action involving an ancillary estate, give different kinds, portions or undivided interests in property to beneficiaries and assign value to all things, and do any distribution or division of my estate or property in cash or in kind.

If a gift including of household items goes to several beneficiaries the executor shall have sole discretion how to divide the gift, taking into account feelings of beneficiaries and myself.

Any executor may any time and in any amount pay debts of mine or my estate they in their sole and absolute discretion finds are valid, enforceable, timely, and fair, including of a last illness, for funeral and related things, and all with no filing or act of court or others.

If any property is distributable under this Will to a minor person, I authorize my executor or other party to make distribution to a custodian for the minor under the Uniform Transfers to Minors Act of Texas or any other state, with any person named in this Will as guardian of the estate as custodian but even if they are available my executor may nominate another person.

Any successor including of an executor or guardian of any type named in this Will shall have all powers, privileges, immunities and exemptions their predecessor had.

Not giving anything or more to my children and other family is intentional and not a mistake.

The residue includes lapsed or failed gifts, insurance paid to the estate, inheritances owed testator, and property testator had power of appointment or testamentary disposition over.

TESTATOR

IN WITNESS WHEREOF, I hereunto subscribe my name and declare, publish, and acknowledge this as my Last Will and Testament as Testator all in the presence of the witnesses signing below, this __ day of _____, 20__.

_____
Testator

WITNESSES

The foregoing instrument was signed, published, and declared by the above Testator in our presence as the Last Will and Testament of such Testator, and we the undersigned Witnesses sign our names hereunto as witnesses at the request and in the presence of the such Testator and in the presence of each other, on this __ day of _____, 20__.

_____   _____
Witness   Address

_____   _____
Witness   Address

CHAPTER 7
FORM 3: SELF-PROVING AFFIDAVIT

FORM 3 IS "SELF-PROVING AFFIDAVIT"

Form 3 in this book is the "Self-Proving Affidavit" form copied exactly from the statutory form found in law at Texas Estates Code section 251.101. Doing this form helps avoid later legal work and also makes it more like a Will will be followed by a court and others.

SELF-PROVING AFFIDAVIT IS OPTIONAL BUT MAY REDUCE LATER WORK

Doing a Self-Proving Affidavit is not required to have a valid Will, but it is recommended and is common. However as said below doing this form can be a hassle, since it requires a notary be present along with the normal 2 witnesses and the person making the Will. But if a Self-Proving Affidavit is not done then usually after a death one witness to the Will signing has to be found and testify in court to show a Will was signed correctly to be legally valid (in some cases other evidence can do this). Some people doing a Will skip a Self-Proving Affidavit because of work, stress, and delay that doing it may involve and since because this form is not required to have a valid Will, but again the Self-Proving Affidavit is recommended.

COMPLETE SELF-PROVING AFFIDAVIT BY ALL SIGNING BEFORE NOTARY

To be valid, a Self-Proving Affidavit must be signed before a notary by the person making a Will and the two witnesses to the Will signing. Often, this is done minutes after a Will is signed, but this can also be done anytime later after a Will signing when everyone is before a notary. Some people do a Will fast and take their time getting everyone before a notary to do the Self-Proving Affidavit. A notary can be found at some banks, insurance agencies, courts, copy places, government offices, business offices, or by hiring a notary from a phonebook (this last option can avoid problems but may require buying other services from the notary). When completed, a Self-Proving Affidavit form should be attached by paperclip or staple to the Will it supports.

FORM 3:
SELF-PROVING AFFIDAVIT

<u>SELF-PROVING AFFIDAVIT</u>

THE STATE OF TEXAS

COUNTY OF _____

      BEFORE ME, the undersigned authority, on this day personally appeared
_____, _____, and _____,
known to me to be the Testator and the witnesses, respectively, whose names are subscribed to
the annexed or foregoing instrument in their respective capacities, and, all of said persons being
by me duly sworn, the said _____, Testator, declared to me and to
the said witnesses in my presence that said instrument is his or her last Will and testament, and
that he or she had willingly made and executed it as his or her free act and deed; and the said
witnesses, each on his or her oath stated to me, in the presence and hearing of the said Testator,
that the said Testator had declared to them that said instrument is his or her last Will and
testament, and that he or she executed same as such and wanted each of them to sign it as a
witness; and upon their oaths each witness stated further that they did sign the same as
witnesses in the presence of the said Testator and at his or her request; that he or she was at that
time eighteen years of age or over (or being under such age, was or had been lawfully married,
or was then a member of the armed forces of the United States, or an auxiliary of the armed
forces of the United States, or the United States Maritime Service) and was of sound mind; and
that each of said witnesses was then at least fourteen years of age.

_____
Testator

_____
Witness

_____
Witness

      SUBSCRIBED AND SWORN TO before me by the said _____,
Testator, and by the said _____ and _____, Witnesses,
this ___ day of _____ A.D. 20___.

      (SEAL)

(Signed) _____
Notary Public, State of Texas

CHAPTER 8
FORM 4: TANGIBLE PERSONAL PROPERTY LIST

FORM LETS PEOPLE WRITE WANTED GIFTS OF SOME PROPERTY

Form 4 lets people write down wanted gifts of tangible personal property to occur after their death, and often is used for less valuable items of clothing, furniture, jewelry, appliances, and tools. Often this form or similar forms are called "Lists", "Gift Lists", or "Gift Memorandum". But the Tangible Personal Property List is not technically legally binding in Texas as explained below.

FORM NOT LEGALLY BINDING BUT FAMILY MAY LATER AGREE TO FOLLOW IT

Form 4 lets people write down gifts of tangible personal property they want to occur after their death. Importantly, this form is not usually legally binding since in Texas gifts and transfers to occur after death usually must be in a Will or similar document. Even if not legally binding, often family and others, who by Will or state law have control of property, do voluntarily later agree to follow any such writings. Family and others are usually free to not follow a list or similar writing. It is recommended people not put valuable property in lists, and usually items worth under $100 are put in a list and given to people who would really appreciate an item. People can do many lists but it is a bit better to do one big list stapled together and signed on one date.

LIST FORM ONLY GIVES "TANGIBLE PERSONAL PROPERTY"

Lists are usually used to gift furniture, clothing, appliances, tools, and jewelry. This book's form only gives "tangible personal property", so only "tangible" property with solid form (not accounts or most investments), only "personal property" so not real property (not buildings or land), and not money (so not coins or paper money even if antiques). Property used in a trade or business usually should not be in a list. Valuable property usually should not be in a list. Examples of list gifts are:

> "Silver Lamp to Amy Smith",
> "Small diamond ring to Kay Coe", and
> "Winter coats and boots to Mary Sue Paulson".

TANGIBLE PERSONAL PROPERTY LIST MUST BE SIGNED AND DATED

To be completed a Tangible Personal Property List form should be signed and dated. To be followed a list must be found after a person's death, and lists are often paperclipped to a Will or kept nearby. A list can be revoked by writing canceled on it, destroying it, or just having it so it is not found after a person's death to be followed.

FORM 4:
TANGIBLE PERSONAL PROPERTY LIST

TANGIBLE PERSONAL PROPERTY LIST

I request but do not require family and other people after my death follow the gifts of property I write below. I understand in this form only tangible personal property should be given, so not land or buildings, not money, and not investments or accounts without a tangible form. A gift written below has no effect if a named recipient does not survive me by 60 days or if a Will specifically gives the property.

PROPERTY ITEMS GIFTED   **NAMES OF RECIPIENTS**

_____   _____

_____   _____

_____   _____

_____   _____

_____   _____

_____   _____

_____   _____

_____   _____

_____   _____

_____   _____

_____   _____

_____   _____

DATE: _____   SIGNED: _____

CHAPTER 9
FORM 5: CODICIL

FORM 5 "CODICIL" FORM CAN BE USED TO CHANGE PARTS OF A WILL

To change parts of an existing Will it is usually best to do a new Will to reduce the chance of confusion about what words are meant. If wanted, one can use a "Codicil" form to change parts of a Will, to add to a Will, or to remove parts of a Will.

IN CODICIL TO CHANGE WILL JUST LIST WORDS TO REMOVE AND TO ADD

In a Codicil form, usually one first writes the words to be removed from a Will, and then one writes the new words to be added to a Will. The Codicil can also be used to add whole new things or remove things. Often the Codicil does simple things that should not be too confusing to others like replacing a beneficiary name, replacing property in a gift, adding or deleting a whole gift, or naming a different person as executor or guardian. These things might be done because people named in a Will have died or no longer need things, or because gifted property in a Will is no longer owned so needs to be replaced.

CODICIL MUST BE SIGNED BEFORE 2 WITNESSES WHO SIGN

To be valid, a Codicil must be signed just like a Will and meet all the normal requirements for a Will signing. Basically, the person making the document must sign before two witnesses who also sign. Witnesses should be "disinterested witnesses", not getting gifts in the Will since acting as witness usually undoes any Will gifts to them (except if under "intestate law" they as close family would get things if there were no Will). When completed, a Codicil document should be kept so it is found with the Will it modifies.

FORM 5:
CODICIL

CODICIL

I, _____, of _____ County, Texas, declare this to be a Codicil to my Will dated _____.

FIRST: I hereby do revoke the part of my Will that reads as follows:

_____

_____

_____

_____

_____.

SECOND: I hereby do add the following part to my Will:

_____

_____

_____

_____

_____.

THIRD: In all other _ I do confirm and republish the above-described Will.

TESTATOR

IN WITNESS WHEREOF, I hereunto subscribe my name and declare, publish, and acknowledge this as my Codicil all in the presence of the witnesses signing below, this __ day of _____, 20__.

_____
Testator

WITNESSES

The foregoing instrument was signed, published, and declared by the above Testator in our presence as the Codicil of such Testator, and we undersigned the Witnesses sign our names hereunto as witnesses at the request and in the presence of the such Testator and in the presence of each other, on this __ day of _____, 20__.

_____   _____
Witness   Address

_____   _____
Witness   Address

CHAPTER 10
FORM 6: MEDICAL POWER OF ATTORNEY

FORM LETS AGENT BE NAMED TO CONTROL HEALTH CARE IN CASE NEEDED

Form 6 is a standard form by the Texas legislature found in law at Texas Health And Safety Code sections 166.163 and 166.164, plus a title and places to sign have been added to satisfy Texas law. This form lets a person be named as Agent to control health care for a person in case needed.

IN FORM CAN NAME "AGENT" TO CONTROL HEALTH CARE IF NEEDED

In the form, a person can be named "Health Care Agent" to control health care if a doctor ever later certifies a person can't control their own care. Often people name for this a spouse, adult child, or friend. By law, if no form is done, the first of any spouse, adult children, parent, or other family can control health care by going to court and being named "Surrogate" (so naming them in the form saves time and money). A person named agent must be at least age 18 and not be someone providing health or residential care. Often, if a child turns 18, they use this form to name a parent as Agent.

IN FORM CAN WRITE HEALTH CARE LIMITATIONS AND INSTRUCTIONS

If wanted, in the form a person can give health care instructions or limitations, which by law all persons must follow in addition to verbal statements a person ever makes while competent. Many people skip instructions to not limit a trusted agent's freedom in likely complex medical situations, or because instructions could be seen as unclear and cause legal problems. Using this form to name an agent, especially if the form also has instructions about end of life matters, may avoid need for a "Directive To Physicians And Family Or Surrogates" (also called a "Living Will") covered in this book's Chapter 11. If several forms give conflicting instructions, the more recent one controls.

COMPLETE FORM BY SIGNING WITH NOTARY OR 2 WITNESSES

To be valid, the Medical Power Of Attorney form's "Disclosure Statement" on page 1 and 2 should be read and signed by the person doing the form. Then, at form end, the person doing the form should sign the form before a notary or, alternatively, before two witnesses over age 18 who then also sign. If using witnesses the one called "First Witness" 1) must not be named agent in the form, 2) must not be related to a person by blood or marriage, 3) must not be owned money or be entitled by Will or by law if there were no Will to anything, 4) must not be attending physician or their employee, and 5) must not work at a health care facility giving care or associated organization. When completed, the form should be shown or copies given to doctors and to health care facility giving care, and the original form should be kept close at hand or given to the named agent.

FORM 6:
MEDICAL POWER OF ATTORNEY

DISCLOSURE STATEMENT

INFORMATION CONCERNING
THE MEDICAL POWER OF ATTORNEY

THIS IS AN IMPORTANT LEGAL DOCUMENT. BEFORE SIGNING THIS DOCUMENT, YOU SHOULD KNOW THESE IMPORTANT FACTS:

Except to the extent you state otherwise, this document gives the person you name as your agent the authority to make any and all health care decisions for you in accordance with your wishes, including your religious and moral beliefs, when you are no longer capable of making them yourself. Because "health care" means any treatment, service, or procedure to maintain, diagnose, or treat your physical or mental condition, your agent has the power to make a broad range of health care decisions for you. Your agent may consent, refuse to consent, or withdraw consent to medical treatment and may make decisions about withdrawing or withholding life-sustaining treatment. Your agent may not consent to voluntary inpatient mental health services, convulsive treatment, psychosurgery, or abortion. A physician must comply with your agent's instructions or allow you to be transferred to another physician.

Your agent's authority begins when your doctor certifies that you lack the competence to make health care decisions.

Your agent is obligated to follow your instructions when making decisions on your behalf. Unless you state otherwise, your agent has the same authority to make decisions about your health care as you would have had.

It is important that you discuss this document with your physician or other health care provider before you sign it to make sure that you understand the nature and range of decisions that may be made on your behalf. If you do not have a physician, you should talk with someone else who is knowledgeable about these issues and can answer your questions. You do not need a lawyer's assistance to complete this document, but if there is anything in this document that you do not understand, you should ask a lawyer to explain it to you.

The person you appoint as agent should be someone you know and trust. The person must be 18 years of age or older or a person under 18 years of age who has had the disabilities of minority removed. If you appoint your health or residential care provider (e.g., your physician or an employee of a home health agency, hospital, nursing home, or residential care home, other than a relative), that person has to choose between acting as your agent or as your health or residential care provider; the law does not permit a person to do both at the same time.

You should inform the person you appoint that you want the person to be your health care agent. You should discuss this document with your agent and your physician and give each a signed copy. You should indicate on the document itself the people and institutions who have signed copies. Your agent is not liable for health care decisions made in good faith on your behalf.

Even after you have signed this document, you have the right to make health care decisions for yourself as long as you are able to do so and treatment cannot be given to you or stopped over your objection. You have the right to revoke the authority granted to your agent by informing your agent or your health or residential care provider orally or in writing or by your execution of a subsequent medical power of attorney. Unless you state otherwise, your appointment of a spouse dissolves on divorce.

This document may not be changed or modified. If you want to make changes in the document, you must make an entirely new one.

You may wish to designate an alternate agent in the event that your agent is unwilling, unable, or ineligible to act as your agent. Any alternate agent you designate has the same authority to make health care decisions for you.

THIS POWER OF ATTORNEY IS NOT VALID UNLESS:
(1) YOU SIGN IT AND HAVE YOUR SIGNATURE ACKNOWLEDGED BEFORE A NOTARY PUBLIC; OR
(2) YOU SIGN IT IN THE PRESENCE OF TWO COMPETENT ADULT WITNESSES. THE FOLLOWING PERSONS MAY NOT ACT AS ONE OF THE WITNESSES:

(1) the person you have designated as your agent;

(2) a person related to you by blood or marriage;

(3) a person entitled to any part of your estate after your death under a will or codicil executed by you or by operation of law;

(4) your attending physician;

(5) an employee of your attending physician;

(6) an employee of a health care facility in which you are a patient if the employee is providing direct patient care to you or is an officer, director, partner, or business office employee of the health care facility or of any parent organization of the health care facility; or

(7) a person who, at the time this power of attorney is executed, has a claim against any part of your estate after your death.

ACKNOWLEDGMENT OF DISCLOSURE STATEMENT

By signing immediately below I agree and state I have received, read, and understood the contents of the above Disclosure Statement prior to executing the Medical Power Of Attorney in this document.

Signature _____

MEDICAL POWER OF ATTORNEY
DESIGNATION OF HEALTH CARE AGENT

I, _____ (insert your name) appoint:

    Name: _____

    Address: _____ Phone: _____

as my agent to make any and all health care decisions for me, except to the extent I state otherwise in this document. This medical power of attorney takes effect if I become unable to make my own health care decisions and this fact is certified in writing by my physician.

LIMITATIONS ON THE DECISION-MAKING AUTHORITY OF MY AGENT ARE AS FOLLOWS: _____

_____

_____

_____

_____

_____

DESIGNATION OF ALTERNATE AGENT.

    (You are not required to designate an alternate agent but you may do so. An alternate agent may make the same health care decisions as the designated agent if the designated agent is unable or unwilling to act as your agent. If the agent designated is your spouse, the designation is automatically revoked by law if your marriage is dissolved.)

    If the person designated as my agent is unable or unwilling to make health care decisions for me, I designate the following persons to serve as my agent to make health care decisions for me as authorized by this document, who serve in the following order:

A. First Alternate Agent

Name: _____

Address: _____

Phone: _____

B. Second Alternate Agent

Name: _____

Address: _____

Phone: _____

The original of this document is kept at:

_____

The following individuals or institutions have signed copies:

    Name: _____ Address: _____

    Name: _____ Address: _____

DURATION.

    I understand that this power of attorney exists indefinitely from the date I execute this document unless I establish a shorter time or revoke the power of attorney. If I am unable to make health care decisions for myself when this power of attorney expires, the authority I have granted my agent continues to exist until the time I become able to make health care decisions for myself.

(IF APPLICABLE) This power of attorney ends on the following date: _____

PRIOR DESIGNATIONS REVOKED.

I revoke any prior medical power of attorney.

ACKNOWLEDGMENT OF DISCLOSURE STATEMENT.

I have been provided with a disclosure statement explaining the effect of this document. I have read and understand that information contained in the disclosure statement.

(YOU MUST DATE AND SIGN THIS POWER OF ATTORNEY. YOU MAY SIGN IT AND HAVE YOU SIGNATURE ACKNOWLEDGED BEFORE A NOTARY PUBLIC OR YOU MAY SIGN IT IN THE PRESENCE OF TWO COMPETENT ADULT WITNESSES.)

SIGNATURE ACKNOWLEDGED BEFORE NOTARY

I sign my name to this medical power of attorney on ___ day of _____ (month, year) at _____ (City and State).

_____ (Signature)   _____ (Print Name)

State of Texas

County of _____

This instrument was acknowledged before me on _____ (date) by _____ (name of person acknowledging).

_____
NOTARY PUBLIC, State of Texas
Notary's printed name: _____
My commission expires: _____

OR

SIGNATURE IN PRESENCE OF TWO COMPETENT ADULT WITNESSES

I sign my name to this medical power of attorney on ___ day of _____ (month, year) at _____ (City and State).

_____ (Signature)   _____ (Print Name)

STATEMENT OF FIRST WITNESS.

I am not the person appointed as agent by this document. I am not related to the principal by blood or marriage. I would not be entitled to any portion of the principal's estate on the principal's death. I am not the attending physician of the principal or an employee of the attending physician. I have no claim against any portion of the principal's estate on the principal's death. Furthermore, if I am an employee of a health care facility in which the principal is a patient, I am not involved in providing direct patient care to the principal and am not an officer, director, partner, or business office employee of the health care facility or of any parent organization of the health care facility.

Signature:_____

Print Name:_____   Date:_____

Address:_____

SIGNATURE OF SECOND WITNESS.

Signature:_____

Print Name:_____   Date:_____

Address:_____

CHAPTER 11
FORM 7: DIRECTIVE TO PHYSICIANS AND FAMILY OR SURROGATES (LIVING WILL)

FORM 7 LETS PERSON CONTROL END OF LIFE MEDICAL ISSUES

Form 7 is a statutory form found in law at Health and Safety Code section 166.033. The form is often called a "Directive" or a "Living Will" since it is like a Will that takes effect during life. A "surrogate" the form refers to is someone given power by a court or doctor over health care.

FORM ORDERS IF NEAR DEATH OR SIMILAR THAT CARE SHOULD STOP

This form takes effect only if a doctor later certifies in writing a person lacks capacity to control their own health care (they can't communicate, can't comprehend, or similar) and, also, they are a) in a "terminal condition" and expected to die within 6 months even with life-sustaining treatment, or b) have an "irreversible condition" so can't care for or make decisions for themselves and are expected to die even with normal life-sustaining treatment. The form has two places to initial to say if in such bad health: "I request that all treatments other than those needed to keep me comfortable be discontinued or withheld and my physician allow me to die as gently as possible". The other form option is to say care goes on no matter what. If a form is not done, family or an agent in charge could order care despite cost, pain, stress, and delay when any benefit is slight. In a form requests can be given like on treatments, doctors, or locations, but many leave this blank to avoid possible problems. A form can be revoked, even if lacking mental facilities, by a verbal or written statement to family or doctors. A form can name two persons to control health care if wanted.

MANY PEOPLE ONLY USE THE MEDICAL POWER OF ATTORNEY FORM

Many people skip this Form 7 and only use a Medical Power of Attorney (Form 6 in this book) to name an agent and give instructions since it covers all medical situations, while Form 7 is only for when clearly near death. Some people use both two forms if family need clear orders to stop care. Doctors do not follow Form 7 if a person or a Health Care Agent can give orders on care.

TO BE VALID SIGN FORM WITH 2 WITNESSES

To be valid Form 7, needs be signed by a person before either a notary, or before 2 witnesses who then also sign. Of the two witnesses, the witness called "Witness 1" cannot be 1) someone with control of health care, 2) related by blood or marriage, 3) be entitled by Will or without a Will under "intestate" law to property or be owed money, 4) be attending physician or their employee, 5) be a health care worker involved in giving care, and 6) be any kind of officer at a facility giving care or any related organization. A person need not use both a notary and the two witnesses.

47

FORM 7:
DIRECTIVE TO PHYSICIANS AND FAMILY
OR SURROGATES (LIVING WILL)

DIRECTIVE TO PHYSICIANS
AND FAMILY OR SURROGATES

Instructions for completing this document:

This is an important legal document known as an Advance Directive. It is designed to help you communicate your wishes about medical treatment at some time in the future when you are unable to make your wishes known because of illness or injury. These wishes are usually based on personal values. In particular, you may want to consider what burdens or hardships of treatment you would be willing to accept for a particular amount of benefit obtained if you were seriously ill.

You are encouraged to discuss your values and wishes with your family or chosen spokesperson, as well as your physician. Your physician, other health care provider, or medical institution may provide you with various resources to assist you in completing your advance directive. Brief definitions are listed below and may aid you in your discussions and advance planning. Initial the treatment choices that best reflect your personal preferences. Provide a copy of your directive to your physician, usual hospital, and family or spokesperson. Consider a periodic review of this document. By periodic review, you can best assure that the directive reflects your preferences.

In addition to this advance directive, Texas law provides for two other types of directives that can be important during a serious illness. These are the Medical Power of Attorney and the Out-of-Hospital Do-Not-Resuscitate Order. You may wish to discuss these with your physician, family, hospital representative, or other advisers. You may also wish to complete a directive related to the donation of organs and tissues.

DIRECTIVE

I, _____, recognize that the best health care is based upon a partnership of trust and communication with my physician. My physician and I will make health care decisions together as long as I am of sound mind and able to make my wishes known. If there comes a time that I am unable to make medical decisions about myself because of illness or injury, I direct that the following treatment preferences be honored:

If, in the judgment of my physician, I am suffering with a terminal condition from which I am expected to die within six months, even with available life-sustaining treatment provided in accordance with prevailing standards of medical care:

_____ **I request that all treatments other than those needed to keep me comfortable be discontinued or withheld and my physician allow me to die as gently as possible; OR**

_____ **I request that I be kept alive in this terminal condition using available life-sustaining treatment. (THIS SELECTION DOES NOT APPLY TO HOSPICE CARE.)**

If, in the judgment of my physician, I am suffering with an irreversible condition so that I cannot care for myself or make decisions for myself and am expected to die without life-sustaining treatment provided in accordance with prevailing standards of care:

_____ I request that all treatments other than those needed to keep me comfortable be discontinued or withheld and my physician allow me to die as gently as possible; OR

_____ I request that I be kept alive in this irreversible condition using available life-sustaining treatment. (THIS SELECTION DOES NOT APPLY TO HOSPICE CARE.)

Additional requests: (After discussion with your physician, you may wish to consider listing particular treatments in this space that you do or do not want in specific circumstances, such as artificial nutrition and fluids, intravenous antibiotics, etc. Be sure to state whether you do or do not want the particular treatment.)

_____

_____

_____

_____

After signing this directive, if my representative or I elect hospice care, I understand and agree that only those treatments needed to keep me comfortable would be provided and I would not be given available life-sustaining treatments.

If I do not have a Medical Power of Attorney, and I am unable to make my wishes known, I designate the following person(s) to make treatment decisions with my physician compatible with my personal values:

1. _____

2. _____

(If a Medical Power of Attorney has been executed, then an agent already has been named and you should not list additional names in this document.)

If the above persons are not available, or if I have not designated a spokesperson, I understand that a spokesperson will be chosen for me following standards specified in the laws of Texas. If, in the judgment of my physician, my death is imminent within minutes to hours, even with the use of all available medical treatment provided within the prevailing standard of care, I acknowledge that all treatments may be withheld or removed except those needed to maintain my comfort. I understand that under Texas law this directive has no effect if I have been diagnosed as pregnant. This directive will remain in effect until I revoke it. No other person may do so.

Signed _____   Date _____

City, County, State of Residence _____

Two competent adult witnesses must sign below, acknowledging the signature of the declarant. The witness designated as Witness 1 may not be a person designated to make a treatment decision for the patient and may not be related to the patient by blood or marriage. This witness may not be entitled to any part of the estate and may not have a claim against the estate of the patient. This witness may not be the attending physician or an employee of the attending physician. If this witness is an employee of a health care facility in which the patient is being cared for, this witness may not be involved in providing direct patient care to the patient. This witness may not be an officer, director, partner, or business office employee of a health care facility in which the patient is being cared for or of any parent organization of the health care facility.

Witness 1 _____   Witness 2 _____

Definitions:

"Artificial nutrition and hydration" means the provision of nutrients or fluids by a tube inserted in a vein, under the skin in the subcutaneous tissues, or in the stomach (gastrointestinal tract).

"Irreversible condition" means a condition, injury, or illness:
(1) that may be treated, but is never cured or eliminated;
(2) that leaves a person unable to care for or make decisions for the person's own self; and
(3) that, without life-sustaining treatment provided in accordance with the prevailing standard of medical care, is fatal.

Explanation: Many serious illnesses such as cancer, failure of major organs (kidney, heart, liver, or lung), and serious brain disease such as Alzheimer's dementia may be considered irreversible early on. There is no cure, but the patient may be kept alive for prolonged periods of time if the patient receives life-sustaining treatments. Late in the course of the same illness, the disease may be considered terminal when, even with treatment, the patient is expected to die. You may wish to consider which burdens of treatment you would be willing to accept in an effort to achieve a particular outcome. This is a very personal decision that you may wish to discuss with your physician, family, or other important persons in your life.

"Life-sustaining treatment" means treatment that, based on reasonable medical judgment, sustains the life of a patient and without which the patient will die. The term includes both life-sustaining medications and artificial life support such as mechanical breathing machines, kidney dialysis treatment, and artificial hydration and nutrition. The term does not include the administration of pain management medication, the performance of a medical procedure necessary to provide comfort care, or any other medical care provided to alleviate a patient's pain.

"Terminal condition" means an incurable condition caused by injury, disease, or illness that according to reasonable medical judgment will produce death within six months, even with available life-sustaining treatment provided in accordance with the prevailing standard of medical care.

Explanation: Many serious illnesses may be considered irreversible early in the course of the illness, but they may not be considered terminal until the disease is fairly advanced. In thinking about terminal illness and its treatment, you again may wish to consider the relative benefits and burdens of treatment and discuss your wishes with your physician, family, or other important persons in your life.

CHAPTER 12
FORM 8: DO-NOT-RESUSCITATE

FORM 8 IS "DO-NOT-RESUSCITATE" FORM

Form 8 is the "Do-Not-Resuscitate" form which is a standard form by the Department of State Health Services. This form is officially called the "Out-Of-Hospital Do-Not-Resuscitate Order" (the "OOH-DNR"). This form basically tells paramedics and others not to try C.P.R. or similar care in places outside a hospital or similar.

DO-NOT-RESUSCITATE FORM CONTROLS EMERGENCY CARE

People in extreme bad health can use this form to show paramedics and others no attempt to restart a heart or breathing (which is "cardiopulmonary resuscitation" or "C.P.R."), no artificial tube feeding, and no other major care should be tried. People, to ensure this form is followed, should keep the form on or near their body, or wear a "bracelet" with form information. Paramedics and others in a hurry often only look for and follow a Do-Not-Resuscitate form, and ignore other forms. By law, a doctor must fill out and sign the Do-Not-Resuscitate form and usually provides the form and explains form treatment options. Normally, a person requests their own Do-Not-Resuscitate form, but if a person is incapacitated a Health Care Agent named to control things in a Medical Power of Attorney or closest family can request this (but such people must follow written or verbal instructions a person has ever given). The Do-Not-Resuscitate form is not followed in hospitals or similar places, where instead people give orders directly to doctors or use other forms like a Medical Power of Attorney or a Living Will (which are Form 6 or Form 7 in this book).

DOCTOR, PERSON, AND 2 WITNESSES OR NOTARY MUST SIGN FORM

To be valid, a Do-Not-Resuscitate form must be a) filled out and signed by a doctor or similar, b) signed by the person doing the form, and c) signed either by two witnesses or alternatively a notary. Witnesses or a notary are not needed if a second doctor also signs the form. If a person is physically too weak to sign, they can ask another person to sign for them, which must be witnessed. If a person doing the form is using witnesses, by law one of the two witnesses 1) must not be a person controlling health care, 2) not be related by blood or marriage to the person, 3) not be entitled by Will or law to part of the person's estate or be owed money, 4) not be attending physician or their employee, and 5) not be an employee or any kind of officer at a place giving care or a related place.

FORM 8:
DO-NOT-RESUSCITATE

Figure: 25 TAC §157.25 (h)(2)

OUT-OF-HOSPITAL DO-NOT-RESUSCITATE (OOH-DNR) ORDER
TEXAS DEPARTMENT OF STATE HEALTH SERVICES

STOP DO NOT RESUSCITATE

This document becomes effective immediately on the date of execution for health care professionals acting in out-of-hospital settings. It remains in effect until the person is pronounced dead by authorized medical or legal authority or the document is revoked. Comfort care will be given as needed.

Person's full legal name _____ Date of birth _____ ☐ Male ☐ Female

A. Declaration of the adult person: I am competent and at least 18 years of age. **I direct that none of the following resuscitation measures be initiated or continued for me:** cardiopulmonary resuscitation (CPR), transcutaneous cardiac pacing, defibrillation, advanced airway management, artificial ventilation.

Person's signature _____ Date _____ Printed name _____

B. Declaration by legal guardian, agent or proxy on behalf of the adult person who is incompetent or otherwise incapable of communication:

I am the: ☐ legal guardian; ☐ agent in a Medical Power of Attorney; OR ☐ proxy in a directive to physicians of the above-noted person who is incompetent or otherwise mentally or physically incapable of communication.

Based upon the known desires of the person, or a determination of the best interest of the person, **I direct that none of the following resuscitation measures be initiated or continued for the person:** cardiopulmonary resuscitation (CPR), transcutaneous cardiac pacing, defibrillation, advanced airway management, artificial ventilation.

Signature _____ Date _____ Printed name _____

C. Declaration by a qualified relative of the adult person who is incompetent or otherwise incapable of communication: I am the above-noted person's:

☐ spouse, ☐ adult child, ☐ parent, OR ☐ nearest living relative, and I am qualified to make this treatment decision under Health and Safety Code §166.088.

To my knowledge the adult person is incompetent or otherwise mentally or physically incapable of communication and is without a legal guardian, agent or proxy. Based upon the known desires of the person or a determination of the best interests of the person, **I direct that none of the following resuscitation measures be initiated or continued for the person:** cardiopulmonary resuscitation (CPR), transcutaneous cardiac pacing, defibrillation, advanced airway management, artificial ventilation.

Signature _____ Date _____ Printed name _____

D. Declaration by physician based on directive to physicians by a person now incompetent or nonwritten communication to the physician by a competent person: I am the above-noted person's attending physician and have:

☐ seen evidence of his/her previously issued directive to physicians by the adult, now incompetent; OR ☐ observed his/her issuance before two witnesses of an OOH-DNR in a nonwritten manner.

I direct that none of the following resuscitation measures be initiated or continued for the person: cardiopulmonary resuscitation (CPR), transcutaneous cardiac pacing, defibrillation, advanced airway management, artificial ventilation.

Attending physician's signature _____ Date _____ Printed name _____ Lic# _____

E. Declaration on behalf of the minor person: I am the minor's: ☐ parent; ☐ legal guardian; OR ☐ managing conservator.

A physician has diagnosed the minor as suffering from a terminal or irreversible condition. **I direct that none of the following resuscitation measures be initiated or continued for the person:** cardiopulmonary resuscitation (CPR), transcutaneous cardiac pacing, defibrillation, advanced airway management, artificial ventilation.

Signature _____ Date _____

Printed name _____

TWO WITNESSES: (See qualifications on backside.) We have witnessed the above-noted competent adult person or authorized declarant making his/her signature above and, if applicable, the above-noted adult person making an OOH-DNR by nonwritten communication to the attending physician.

Witness 1 signature _____ Date _____ Printed name _____

Witness 2 signature _____ Date _____ Printed name _____

Notary in the State of Texas and County of _____. The above noted person personally appeared before me and signed the above noted declaration on this date: _____

Signature & seal: _____ Notary's printed name: _____ Notary Seal

[Note: Notary cannot acknowledge the witnessing of the person making an OOH-DNR order in a nonwritten manner]

PHYSICIAN'S STATEMENT: I am the attending physician of the above-noted person and have noted the existence of this order in the person's medical records. **I direct health care professionals acting in out-of-hospital settings, including a hospital emergency department, not to initiate or continue for the person:** cardiopulmonary resuscitation (CPR), transcutaneous cardiac pacing, defibrillation, advanced airway management, artificial ventilation.

Physician's signature _____ Date _____

Printed name _____ License # _____

F. Directive by two physicians on behalf of the adult, who is incompetent or unable to communicate and without guardian, agent, proxy or relative: The person's specific wishes are unknown, but resuscitation measures are, in reasonable medical judgment, considered ineffective or are otherwise not in the best interests of the person. **I direct health care professionals acting in out-of-hospital settings, including a hospital emergency department, not to initiate or continue for the person:** cardiopulmonary resuscitation (CPR), transcutaneous cardiac pacing, defibrillation, advanced airway management, artificial ventilation.

Attending physician's signature _____ Date _____ Printed name _____ Lic# _____

Signature of second physician _____ Date _____ Printed name _____ Lic# _____

Physician's electronic or digital signature must meet criteria listed in Health and Safety Code §166.082(c).

All persons who have signed above must sign below, acknowledging that this document has been properly completed.

Person's signature _____ Guardian/Agent/Proxy/Relative signature _____

Attending physician's signature _____ Second physician's signature _____

Witness 1 signature _____ Witness 2 signature _____ Notary's signature _____

This document or a copy thereof must accompany the person during his/her medical transport.

INSTRUCTIONS FOR ISSUING AN OOH-DNR ORDER

PURPOSE: The Out-of-Hospital Do-Not-Resuscitate (OOH-DNR) Order on reverse side complies with Health and Safety Code (HSC), Chapter 166 for use by qualified persons or their authorized representatives to direct health care professionals to forgo resuscitation attempts and to permit the person to have a natural death with peace and dignity. This Order does NOT affect the provision of other emergency care, including comfort care.

APPLICABILITY: This OOH-DNR Order applies to health care professionals in out-of-hospital settings, including physicians' offices, hospital clinics and emergency departments.

IMPLEMENTATION: A competent adult person, at least 18 years of age, or the person's authorized representative or qualified relative may execute or issue an OOH-DNR Order. The person's attending physician will document existence of the Order in the person's permanent medical record. The OOH-DNR Order may be executed as follows:

Section A - If an adult person is competent and at least 18 years of age, he/she will sign and date the Order in Section A.

Section B - If an adult person is incompetent or otherwise mentally or physically incapable of communication and has either a legal guardian, agent in a medical power of attorney, or proxy in a directive to physicians, the guardian, agent, or proxy may execute the OOH-DNR Order by signing and dating it in Section B.

Section C - If the adult person is incompetent or otherwise mentally or physically incapable of communication and does not have a guardian, agent, or proxy, then a qualified relative may execute the OOH-DNR Order by signing and dating it in Section C.

Section D - If the person is incompetent and his/her attending physician has seen evidence of the person's previously issued proper directive to physicians or observed the person competently issue an OOH-DNR Order in a nonwritten manner, the physician may execute the Order on behalf of the person by signing and dating it in Section D.

Section E - If the person is a **minor** (less than 18 years of age), **who has been diagnosed by a physician as suffering from a terminal or irreversible condition**, then the minor's parents, legal guardian, or managing conservator may execute the OOH-DNR Order by signing and dating it in Section E.

Section F - If an adult person is incompetent or otherwise mentally or physically incapable of communication and does not have a guardian, agent, proxy, or available qualified relative to act on his/her behalf, then the attending physician may execute the OOH-DNR Order by signing and dating it in Section F with concurrence of a second physician (signing it in Section F) who is not involved in the treatment of the person or who is not a representative of the ethics or medical committee of the health care facility in which the person is a patient.

In addition, the OOH-DNR Order must be signed and dated by two competent adult witnesses, who have witnessed either the competent adult person making his/her signature in section A, or authorized declarant making his/her signature in either sections B, C, or E, and if applicable, have witnessed a competent adult person making an OOH-DNR Order by nonwritten communication to the attending physician, who must sign in Section D and also the physician's statement section. Optionally, a competent adult person or authorized declarant may sign the OOH-DNR Order in the presence of a notary public. However, a notary cannot acknowledge witnessing the issuance of an OOH-DNR in a nonwritten manner, which must be observed and only can be acknowledged by two qualified witnesses. Witness or notary signatures are not required when two physicians execute the OOH-DNR Order in section F. The original or a copy of a fully and properly completed OOH-DNR Order or the presence of an OOH-DNR device on a person is sufficient evidence of the existence of the original OOH-DNR Order and either one shall be honored by responding health care professionals.

REVOCATION: An OOH-DNR Order may be revoked at ANY time by the person, person's authorized representative, or physician who executed the order. Revocation can be by verbal communication to responding health care professionals, destruction of the OOH-DNR Order, or removal of all OOH-DNR identification devices from the person.

AUTOMATIC REVOCATION: An OOH-DNR Order is automatically revoked for a person known to be pregnant or in the case of unnatural or suspicious circumstances.

DEFINITIONS

Attending Physician: A physician, selected by or assigned to a person, with primary responsibility for the person's treatment and care and is licensed by the Texas Medical Board, or is properly credentialed and holds a commission in the uniformed services of the United States and is serving on active duty in this state. [HSC §166.002(12)].

Health Care Professional: Means physicians, nurses, physician assistants and emergency medical services personnel, and, unless the context requires otherwise, includes hospital emergency department personnel. [HSC §166.081(5)]

Qualified Relative: A person meeting requirements of HSC §166.088. It states that an adult relative may execute an OOH-DNR Order on behalf of an adult person who has not executed or issued an OOH-DNR Order and is incompetent or otherwise mentally or physically incapable of communication and is without a legal guardian, agent in a medical power of attorney, or proxy in a directive to physicians, and the relative is available from one of the categories in the following priority: 1) person's spouse; 2) person's reasonably available adult children; 3) the person's parents; or, 4) the person's nearest living relative. Such qualified relative may execute an OOH-DNR Order on such described person's behalf.

Qualified Witnesses: Both witnesses must be competent adults, who have witnessed the competent adult person making his/her signature in section A, or person's authorized representatives making his/her signature in either Sections B, C, or E on the OOH-DNR Order, or if applicable, have witnessed the competent adult person making an OOH-DNR by nonwritten communication to the attending physician, who signs in Section D. Optionally, a competent adult person, guardian, agent, proxy, or qualified relative may sign the OOH-DNR Order in the presence of a notary instead of two qualified witnesses. Witness or notary signatures are not required when two physicians execute the order by signing Section F. One of the witnesses must meet the qualifications in HSC §166.003(2), which requires that at least one of the witnesses not: (1) be designated by the person to make a treatment decision; (2) be related to the person by blood or marriage; (3) be entitled to any part of the person's estate after the person's death either under a will or by law; (4) have a claim at the time of the issuance of the OOH-DNR against any part of the person's estate after the person's death; or, (5) be the attending physician; (6) be an employee of the attending physician or (7) an employee of a health care facility in which the person is a patient if the employee is providing direct patient care to the patient or is an officer, director, partner, or business office employee of the health care facility or any parent organization of the health care facility.

Report problems with this form to the Texas Department of State Health Services (DSHS) or order OOH-DNR Order/forms or identification devices at (512) 834-6700.

Declarant's, Witness', Notary's, or Physician's electronic or digital signature must meet criteria outlined in HSC §166.011

CHAPTER 13
FORM 9: STATUTORY DURABLE
POWER OF ATTORNEY

FORM 9 IS "STATUTORY DURABLE POWER OF ATTORNEY" FORM

Form 9 is a standard form by the Texas legislature found in law at Estates Code section 752.051. This form is often called a "Power Of Attorney" for short. Most banks and others in Texas should know this statutory form, but some banks and others may have their own forms.

FORM LETS PERSON SHARE FINANCIAL POWER WITH AGENT

The Power of Attorney form lets a person at least age 18 share during life what powers they (as "Principal") want to share with another person, like a trusted spouse, relative, or friend (called the "Agent" or "Attorney-in-Fact"). This is usually done if a person needs help because they will be away or are sick, tired, or just too busy. A Power of Attorney form often gives power over financial matters such as over accounts, loans, real estate and other property, and records. Using this form may avoid need for more serious steps like guardianship or nursing home. Forms some lawyers write are "Springing Power of Attorney" forms that take effect only when an event occurs like illness, but such forms can cause legal problems and are not recommended. Whenever using the form an agent should identify himself or herself, like "James Eric Smith as Attorney in Fact for Evelyn Grace Brown".

IN FORM INITIAL POWERS, GIVE INSTRUCTIONS, AND PICK IF "DURABLE"

By having spots to initial, the Power of Attorney form lets a person pick what powers to give (or a person can select option "N" to give all listed powers). Most people give as much power as possible to avoid possible legal problems, and banks and others will not act unless things are clear. The form also has a blank place for instructions or additional powers to be given. Many people try to give as much power as possible in a Power of Attorney by writing under instructions a thing like:

> "I declare this document to be a general power of attorney and my agent (attorney-in-fact) shall have power and authority to perform or take any action I could do if I were personally present."

Some people write to make clear power is given over safety deposit boxes, particular years state or federal taxes, and over specific real estate. Power over health care cannot be given in a normal Power of Attorney form. A Power of Attorney can be "Durable" if, to be more helpful, people want it to continue even if a person is later incapacitated or disabled, and in the form a person must cross out the option they don't want about durability.

DUTIES EXIST FOR AGENT WHO CANNOT GIFT AND DO SOME ACTIONS

A Power of Attorney form lets an agent do dangerous things like sell the principal's property, access accounts, borrow money, and sign for and bind the principal. To help, the law imposes on an agent a legal duty to act in the "best interests" of the principal, keep records, not mix in their money and property, and follow all known wishes, but any misconduct is often not noticed until too late. The law is complex, but it is usually improper to use a Power of Attorney form to gift away things or do unusual actions, and if this might be done a lawyer may be needed.

TO COMPLETE FORM SIGN BEFORE NOTARY

To be valid, the Statutory Durable Power Of Attorney form must be signed by a person doing the form before a notary. The form, once signed, can be kept by a person until needed, given to a spouse or another person to safeguard, or given to the named agent to use when needed. The form can be revoked anytime by a writing or verbal statement made to named agent (and then banks and others should be told of revocation or they can continue to rely on a form they saw). A copy of the form is as valid as the signed original in most cases. A spouse who is named agent, who is then divorced, loses their power to act unless the form says otherwise.

FORM 9:
STATUTORY DURABLE POWER OF ATTORNEY

STATUTORY DURABLE POWER OF ATTORNEY

NOTICE: THE POWERS GRANTED BY THIS DOCUMENT ARE BROAD AND SWEEPING. THEY ARE EXPLAINED IN THE DURABLE POWER OF ATTORNEY ACT, SUBTITLE P, TITLE 2, ESTATES CODE. IF YOU HAVE ANY QUESTIONS ABOUT THESE POWERS, OBTAIN COMPETENT LEGAL ADVICE. THIS DOCUMENT DOES NOT AUTHORIZE ANYONE TO MAKE MEDICAL AND OTHER HEALTH-CARE DECISIONS FOR YOU. YOU MAY REVOKE THIS POWER OF ATTORNEY IF YOU LATER WISH TO DO SO.

You should select someone you trust to serve as your agent (attorney in fact). Unless you specify otherwise, generally the agent's (attorney in fact's) authority will continue until:

       (1) you die or revoke the power of attorney;

       (2) your agent (attorney in fact) resigns or is unable to act for you; or

       (3) a guardian is appointed for your estate.

I, _____ (insert your name and address), appoint _____ (insert the name and address of the person appointed) as my agent (attorney in fact) to act for me in any lawful way with respect to all of the following powers that I have initialed below.

TO GRANT ALL OF THE FOLLOWING POWERS, INITIAL THE LINE IN FRONT OF (N) AND IGNORE THE LINES IN FRONT OF THE OTHER POWERS LISTED IN (A) THROUGH (M).

TO GRANT A POWER, YOU MUST INITIAL THE LINE IN FRONT OF THE POWER YOU ARE GRANTING.

TO WITHHOLD A POWER, DO NOT INITIAL THE LINE IN FRONT OF THE POWER. YOU MAY, BUT DO NOT NEED TO, CROSS OUT EACH POWER WITHHELD.

_____ (A)   Real property transactions;

_____ (B)   Tangible personal property transactions;

_____ (C)   Stock and bond transactions;

_____ (D)   Commodity and option transactions;

_____ (E)   Banking and other financial institution transactions;

_____ (F)   Business operating transactions;

_____ (G)   Insurance and annuity transactions;

_____ (H)   Estate, trust, and other beneficiary transactions;

_____ (I)   Claims and litigation;

_____ (J)   Personal and family maintenance;

_____ (K)   Benefits from social security, Medicare, Medicaid, or other governmental programs or civil or military service;

_____ (L)   Retirement plan transactions;

_____ (M)   Tax matters;

_____ (N)   ALL OF THE POWERS LISTED IN (A) THROUGH (M). YOU DO NOT HAVE TO INITIAL THE LINE IN FRONT OF ANY OTHER POWER IF YOU INITIAL LINE (N).

SPECIAL INSTRUCTIONS:

Special instructions applicable to gifts (initial in front of the following sentence to have it apply):

_____ I grant my agent (attorney in fact) the power to apply my property to make gifts outright to or for the benefit of a person, including by the exercise of a presently exercisable general power of appointment held by me, except that the amount of a gift to an individual may not exceed the amount of annual exclusions allowed from the federal gift tax for the calendar year of the gift.

ON THE FOLLOWING LINES YOU MAY GIVE SPECIAL INSTRUCTIONS LIMITING OR EXTENDING THE POWERS GRANTED TO YOUR AGENT.

_____

_____

_____

_____

_____

_____

_____

_____

_____

UNLESS YOU DIRECT OTHERWISE ABOVE, THIS POWER OF ATTORNEY IS EFFECTIVE IMMEDIATELY AND WILL CONTINUE UNTIL IT IS REVOKED. CHOOSE ONE OF THE FOLLOWING ALTERNATIVES BY CROSSING OUT THE ALTERNATIVE NOT CHOSEN:

(A)   This power of attorney is not affected by my subsequent disability or incapacity.

(B)   This power of attorney becomes effective upon my disability or incapacity.

YOU SHOULD CHOOSE ALTERNATIVE (A) IF THIS POWER OF ATTORNEY IS TO BECOME EFFECTIVE ON THE DATE IT IS EXECUTED.

IF NEITHER (A) NOR (B) IS CROSSED OUT, IT WILL BE ASSUMED THAT YOU CHOSE ALTERNATIVE (A).

If Alternative (B) is chosen and a definition of my disability or incapacity is not contained in this power of attorney, I shall be considered disabled or incapacitated for purposes of this power of attorney if a physician certifies in writing at a date later than the date this power of attorney is executed that, based on the physician's medical examination of me, I am mentally incapable of managing my financial affairs. I authorize the physician who examines me for this purpose to disclose my physical or mental condition to another person for purposes of this power of attorney. A third party who accepts this power of attorney is fully protected from any action taken under this power of attorney that is based on the determination made by a physician of my disability or incapacity.

I agree that any third party who receives a copy of this document may act under it. Revocation of the durable power of attorney is not effective as to a third party until the third party receives actual notice of the revocation. I agree to indemnify the third party for any claims that arise against the third party because of reliance on this power of attorney.

If any agent named by me dies, becomes legally disabled, resigns, or refuses to act, I name the following (each to act alone and successively, in the order named) as successor(s) to that agent: _____.

Signed this ___ day of _____, 20___.

_____
(your signature)

State of Texas

County of _____

This document was acknowledged before me on _____(date) by

_____ (name of principal).

_____
(signature of notarial officer)

(Seal, if any, of notary)   _____
(printed name)
My commission expires: _____

IMPORTANT INFORMATION FOR AGENT (ATTORNEY IN FACT)

Agent's Duties
When you accept the authority granted under this power of attorney, you establish a "fiduciary" relationship with the principal. This is a special legal relationship that imposes on you legal duties that continue until you resign or the power of attorney is terminated or revoked by the principal or by operation of law. A fiduciary duty generally includes the duty to:
 (1)   act in good faith;
 (2)   do nothing beyond the authority granted in this power of attorney;
 (3)   act loyally for the principal's benefit;

(4)   avoid conflicts that would impair your ability to act in the principal's best interest; and

(5)   disclose your identity as an agent or attorney in fact when you act for the principal by writing or printing the name of the principal and signing your own name as "agent" or "attorney in fact" in the following manner:

(Principal's Name) by (Your Signature) as Agent (or as Attorney in Fact)

In addition, the Durable Power of Attorney Act (Subtitle P, Title 2, Estates Code) requires you to:

(1)   maintain records of each action taken or decision made on behalf of the principal;

(2)   maintain all records until delivered to the principal, released by the principal, or discharged by a court; and

(3)   if requested by the principal, provide an accounting to the principal that, unless otherwise directed by the principal or otherwise provided in the Special Instructions, must include:

      (A)   the property belonging to the principal that has come to your knowledge or into your possession;

      (B)   each action taken or decision made by you as agent or attorney in fact;

      (C)   a complete account of receipts, disbursements, and other actions of you as agent or attorney in fact that includes the source and nature of each receipt, disbursement, or action, with receipts of principal and income shown separately;

      (D)   a listing of all property over which you have exercised control that includes an adequate description of each asset and the asset's current value, if known to you;

      (E)   the cash balance on hand and the name and location of the depository at which the cash balance is kept;

      (F)   each known liability;

      (G)   any other information and facts known to you as necessary for a full and definite understanding of the exact condition of the property belonging to the principal; and

      (H)   all documentation regarding the principal's property.

Termination of Agent's Authority

You must stop acting on behalf of the principal if you learn of any event that terminates this power of attorney or your authority under this power of attorney. An event that terminates this power of attorney or your authority to act under this power of attorney includes:

(1)   the principal's death;

(2)   the principal's revocation of this power of attorney or your authority;

(3)   the occurrence of a termination event stated in this power of attorney;

(4)   if you are married to the principal, the dissolution of your marriage by court decree of divorce or annulment;

(5)   the appointment and qualification of a permanent guardian of the principal's estate; or

(6)   if ordered by a court, the suspension of this power of attorney on the appointment and qualification of a temporary guardian until the date the term of the temporary guardian expires.

Liability of Agent

The authority granted to you under this power of attorney is specified in the Durable Power of Attorney Act (Subtitle P, Title 2, Estates Code). If you violate the Durable Power of Attorney Act or act beyond the authority granted, you may be liable for any damages caused by the violation or subject to prosecution for misapplication of property by a fiduciary under Chapter 32 of the Texas Penal Code.

THE ATTORNEY IN FACT OR AGENT, BY ACCEPTING OR ACTING UNDER THE APPOINTMENT, ASSUMES THE FIDUCIARY AND OTHER LEGAL RESPONSIBILITIES OF AN AGENT.

CHAPTER 14
FORM 10: AUTHORIZATION AGREEMENT FOR NONPARENT RELATIVE (OVER CHILD)

FORM LETS PARENT SHARE POWER OVER CHILD WITH CERTAIN RELATIVES

Form 10 is a standard form by the Texas Department of Family and Protective Services and it lets a parent or similar share power over a child with close family so they can help control things.

FORM LETS BROAD POWER OVER CHILD BE GIVEN ONLY TO RELATIVE

The law and Form 10 lets parents share power over a child with: a) grandparent, b) child's aunt or uncle, or c) a child's adult brother or sister (called "siblings"). This form is often done if a child is away from parents and staying with family for travel, school, health care, or parent incarceration. Power given is broad and includes medical and dental care, psychological treatment, immunization, health or car insurance, school or daycare control and enrollment, extracurricular or sport activities, drivers license and IDs, employment, and public benefits. Power over a child's property, marriage, adoption, abortion, and some contraception is not given. A parent can anytime reclaim a child and revoke a form by saying so verbally or in writing to family given power, and then usually they tell schools, doctors, and others to no longer follow a form they saw. Both two parents usually sign a form, and any non-signing parent usually must be sent by certified mail a form copy in 10 days.

FORM IS SIGNED BY PARENTS AND NAMED RELATIVE BEFORE NOTARY

The form is signed before a notary by one or two parents and the relative given power, but everyone can sign at different times. The form can be kept until needed or given to the agent.

FAMILY OR NON-FAMILY CAN GET POWER OVER JUST CHILD'S HEALTH CARE

Using form 10 (explained above) to give power over a child to a relative is recommended since this form is well known and relatives usually can be trusted. However, Texas law also lets power over just a child's health care be given to a non-relative or to a school. A simple writing to do this can be like:

"AUTHORIZATION FOR CONTROL AND CONSENT TO CHILD'S TREATMENT
I _____ am the parent of _____ a minor child born on _____, and I have power to consent to medical and related treatment of said child, and I hereby authorize _____ (who is a person with actual care, control, and possession of said child) to consent to medical, dental, psychological, surgical and related treatment of said child, pursuant to Texas Family Code section 32.001 (Consent by Non-parent) and related laws. Under this authorization no emergency or degree of possible harm is needed, I agree to pay for treatment provided, and I will indemnify and hold harmless from claim or expense any party giving treatment except for negligence. Dated:_____ Signed: _____ "

FORM 10:
AUTHORIZATION AGREEMENT FOR
NONPARENT RELATIVE (OVER CHILD)

AUTHORIZATION AGREEMENT
FOR NONPARENT RELATIVE OR
VOLUNTARY CAREGIVER

This authorization agreement is made in conformance with Chapter 34 of the Texas Family Code concerning the following Child:

Child's Full Name:
Date of Birth:

Parent completing this form:

Full Name:
Physical Address:
Telephone Number:
Other contact information:

Child's other parent:

Full Name:
Physical Address:
Telephone Number:
Other contact information:

Parent voluntarily authorizes the following relative or Parental Child Safety Placement voluntary caregiver to make certain decisions regarding the child, as listed on the next page of this authorization agreement.

Name:
Relationship to Child (check one):   Child's Grandparent ☐   Child's Adult Sibling ☐   Child's Aunt or Uncle ☐   Parental Child Safety Placement Voluntary Caregiver in accordance with Child Protective Services ☐
Physical Address:
Telephone Number:
Other contact information:

PARENT AND RELATIVE OR VOLUNTARY CAREGIVER UNDERSTAND THAT THEY ARE REQUIRED BY LAW TO IMMEDIATELY PROVIDE EACH OTHER WITH INFORMATION REGARDING ANY CHANGE IN THE OTHER PARTY'S ADDRESS OR CONTACT INFORMATION.

Parent authorizes the above named relative or voluntary caregiver to perform the following acts in regard to the child and the relative or voluntary caregiver assumes the responsibility of performing these functions:

(1) To authorize medical, dental, psychological, surgical treatment, and immunization of the child, including executing any consents or authorizations for the release of information as required by law relating to the treatment or immunization;

(2) To obtain and maintain health insurance coverage for the child and automobile insurance coverage for the child, if appropriate;

(3) To enroll the child in a day-care program or public or private preschool, primary or secondary school;

(4) To authorize the child to participate in age-appropriate extracurricular, civic, social, or recreational activities, including athletic activities;

(5) To authorize the child to obtain a learner's permit, driver's license, or state-issued identification card;

(6) To authorize employment of the child; and

(7) To apply for and receive public benefits on behalf of the child.

(8) This authorization agreement does not confer on the relative or voluntary caregiver of the child the right to authorize the performance of an abortion on the child or the administration of emergency contraception to the child

To the best of the parent's and the relative's or voluntary caregiver's knowledge (check if applicable):

☐ **This child is not the subject of a current (pre-existing) valid authorization agreement, and no parent, guardian, custodian, licensed child-placing agency or other agency makes any claim to actual physical possession or care, custody or control of the child that is inconsistent with this authorization agreement.**

To the best of the parent's and the relative's or voluntary caregiver's knowledge (choose one from below):

☐ **THERE IS NO COURT INVOLVEMENT WITH THIS CHILD**
All of the following statements must apply:
- There is no court order or pending suit affecting the parent-child relationship concerning the child.
- There is no pending litigation in any court concerning custody, possession, or placement of the child or access to or visitation with the child.
- The court does not have continuing jurisdiction concerning the child.

☐ **THIS CHILD HAS BEEN THE SUBJECT OF A COURT ACTION**
The court with continuing jurisdiction concerning the child has given written approval for the execution of the authorization agreement accompanied by the following information:
- The county in which the court is located;
- The number of the court; and
- The cause number in which the order was issued or the litigation is pending.
Please staple a copy of the court's order to this agreement.

WARNINGS AND DISCLOSURES

This authorization agreement is an important legal document. The parent and the relative or voluntary caregiver must read all of the warnings and disclosures before signing this authorization agreement.

The parent and relative are not required to consult an attorney but are advised to do so.

A parent's rights as a parent may be adversely affected by placing or leaving the parent's child with another person.

This authorization agreement does not confer on the relative or voluntary caregiver the rights of a managing or possessory conservator or legal guardian.

A parent who is a party to this authorization agreement may terminate the authorization agreement and resume custody, possession, care, and control of the child on demand and at any time the parent may request the return of the child.

Failure by the relative or voluntary caregiver to return the child to the parent immediately on request may have criminal and civil consequences.

Under other applicable law, the relative or voluntary caregiver may be liable for certain expenses relating to the child in the relative's or voluntary caregiver's care, but the parent still retains the parental obligation to support the child.

In certain circumstances, this authorization agreement may not be entered into without written permission of the court. Examples of when court permission must be granted include when a court has entered a previous order granting custody or establishing a child support obligation.

This authorization agreement may be terminated by certain court orders affecting the child.

This authorization agreement does not supersede, invalidate, or terminate any prior authorization agreement regarding the child.

This authorization agreement is void if a prior authorization agreement regarding the child is in effect and has not expired or been terminated.

MAILING REQUIREMENTS:
When both parents do not sign the parent authorization agreement, a copy of the agreement MUST be mailed to the non-signing parent, unless that parent is deceased or has had his or her parental rights terminated. This authorization agreement **is void** unless:
1. The parties mail a copy of this agreement to a non-signing parent **not later than the 10th day** after the date the authorization agreement is signed, **by certified or international registered mail**, as applicable, *return receipt requested*.
2. If the parties do not receive a response from the non-signing parent before the 20th day after the date the copy of the agreement is mailed, the parties must mail a second copy of the agreement **by first class mail or international first class mail**, as applicable, to the parent **not later than the 45th day** after the date the authorization agreement is signed.

EXCEPTION TO MAILING REQUIREMENTS:
If a parent who did not sign the authorization agreement **does not have court-ordered possession of or access to the child who is the subject of the agreement**, the parent who is a party to the agreement does not have to mail a copy of the agreement to the non-signing parent if either of the following circumstances applies:
1. A protective order has been issued against the non-signing parent as provided under Chapter 85 of the Texas Family Code or under a similar law of another state for committing an act of family violence (as defined by Section 71.004 of the Texas Family Code) against the parent

who signed the agreement or any child of the parent who signed the agreement; or

2. The non-signing parent has been convicted of any of the following criminal offenses against the parent who signed the agreement or any child of the parent who signed the agreement:
   - any offense under Title 5 of the Texas Penal Code (including murder, homicide, kidnapping, assault and sexual assault); or
   - any other criminal offense in Texas or any other state if the offense involves a violent act or prohibited sexual conduct.

This authorization agreement (select one of the following two):

☐ Expires on this date: OR

☐ Is valid until revoked in writing by either party

In addition, check here if you want the agreement to continue in effect after your death or during any period of incapacity. ☐

Execution of a subsequent authorization agreement does not by itself supersede, invalidate, or terminate a prior authorization agreement.

By signing below, parent and the relative or voluntary caregiver acknowledge that they have each read this authorization agreement carefully, are entering into the authorization agreement voluntarily, and have read and understand all of the Warnings and Disclosures included in this authorization agreement.

PARENT
Printed name:

SUBSCRIBED AND ACKNOWLEDGED BEFORE ME on this _____ day of _____, 20_____.

_____
Notary Public in and for the State of TEXAS

PARENT**
Printed name:

SUBSCRIBED AND ACKNOWLEDGED BEFORE ME on this _____ day of _____, 20_____.

_____
Notary Public in and for the State of TEXAS

RELATIVE OR VOLUNTARY CAREGIVER
Printed name:

SUBSCRIBED AND ACKNOWLEDGED BEFORE ME on this _____ day of _____, 20_____.

_____
Notary Public in and for the State of TEXAS

CHAPTER 15
FORM 11: APPOINTMENT OF AGENT TO CONTROL DISPOSITION OF REMAINS

FORM 11 LETS ORDERS BE GIVEN AND PERSON NAMED TO CONTROL BODY

Form 11 is a standard form written by the Texas legislature and found in law at Texas Health And Safety Code section 711.002. It lets a person name someone to control and give instructions about their funeral, burial, and other handling of their dead body.

USE FORM TO PICK PERSON TO CONTROL FUNERAL, BURIAL, AND MORE

Form 9 lets a person at least age 18 appoint an "Agent" to control their bodily remains and related matters. This is done if a person does not want a spouse, adult child, or other family to do this, as Texas law provides if no form is done. Some people name a friend to control things, since decisions come when family is in grief and they may not pick wisely or may overspend. In case the first named person cannot serve, the form allows "Successors" to be named to act if needed. Texas law lets people cover funeral wishes in other documents (like a Will), so people should make sure all documents say the same thing. If people die in military service, any military form done controls.

CAN GIVE INSTRUCTIONS ABOUT FUNERAL AND BURIAL

In the form, there is spaces to give instructions people must follow (like locations, funeral and graveside and other ceremonies, or items wanted like caskets or tombstones), but many skip this. Some people just reassure family low cost is wanted, like, "I want an affordable funeral and burial". If there are no written instructions, the person in charge (either a person named in the form or closest family) decides what to do. The estate of a decedent will pay costs, but businesses may ask family to promise to pay if needed, and under Texas law, an Agent named in the form can be liable in some cases. Pre-paid funeral and other contracts decedent made usually must be followed.

DO FORM BY PERSON SIGNING BEFORE NOTARY AND AGENT LATER SIGNS

To be valid, the person doing the form before a notary should sign the Appointment Of Agent To Control Disposition Of Remains form, and later the Agent and any Successor Agents must sign before they act. When completed, the form should be held in a place it will be quickly found within 1 or 2 days of death, or the form can be given to a spouse, friend, or agent to hold.

FORM 11:
APPOINTMENT OF AGENT
TO CONTROL DISPOSITION OF REMAINS

APPOINTMENT OF AGENT
TO CONTROL DISPOSITION OF REMAINS

I, _____,
(your name and address)

being of sound mind, willfully and voluntarily make known my desire that, upon my death, the disposition of my remains shall be controlled by _____
(name of agent)

in accordance with Section 711.002 of the Health and Safety Code and, with respect to that subject only, I hereby appoint such person as my agent (attorney-in-fact).

All decisions made by my agent with respect to the disposition of my remains, including cremation, shall be binding.

SPECIAL DIRECTIONS: Set forth below are any special directions limiting the power granted to my agent:

_____
_____
_____
_____
_____

AGENT:

Name: _____

Address: _____

Telephone Number: _____

Acceptance of Appointment: _____
(signature of agent)

Date of Signature: _____

SUCCESSORS: If my agent dies, becomes legally disabled, resigns, or refuses to act, I hereby appoint the following persons (each to act alone and successively, in the order named) to serve as my agent (attorney-in-fact) to control the disposition of my remains as authorized by this document:

1. First Successor

Name: _____

Address: _____

Telephone Number: _____

Acceptance of Appointment: _____
(signature of first successor)

Date of Signature: _____

2. Second Successor

Name: _____

Address: _____

Telephone Number: _____

Acceptance of Appointment: _____

(signature of second successor)

Date of Signature: _____

DURATION: This appointment becomes effective upon my death.

PRIOR APPOINTMENTS REVOKED: I hereby revoke any prior appointment of any person to control the disposition of my remains.

RELIANCE: I hereby agree that any cemetery organization, business operating a crematory or columbarium or both, funeral director or embalmer, or funeral establishment who receives a copy of this document may act under it. Any modification or revocation of this document is not effective as to any such party until that party receives actual notice of the modification or revocation. No such party shall be liable because of reliance on a copy of this document.

ASSUMPTION: THE AGENT, AND EACH SUCCESSOR AGENT, BY ACCEPTING THIS APPOINTMENT, ASSUMES THE OBLIGATIONS PROVIDED IN, AND IS BOUND BY THE PROVISIONS OF, SECTION 711.002 OF THE HEALTH AND SAFETY CODE.

Signed this _____ day of _____ , 20_____.

_____

(your signature)

State of _____

County of _____

This document was acknowledged before me on _____ (date) by
_____ (name of principal).

_____

signature of notarial officer

(seal, if any, of notary) _____

(printed name) _____

My commission expires: _____

APPENDIX A:
HOW TO DOWNLOAD LEGAL FORMS

TO GET FORMS PEOPLE CAN (1) DOWNLOAD FORMS FREE AS EXPLAINED ON THIS PAGE, OR (2) PHOTOCOPY BOOK PAGES. BOOK BUYERS ARE AUTHORIZED TO DOWNLOAD AND COPY FORMS FOR THEIR OWN AND THEIR FAMILY'S USE.

FILES TO DOWNLOAD ARE IN BOTH:
1) PDF FORMAT WHERE NO CHANGES CAN BE MADE BUT IT CAN BE PRINTED, AND
2) WORD FORMAT WHERE CHANGES CAN BE MADE BY TYPING IN WORDS AND IT CAN BE PRINTED.

DOWNLOAD FORMS AT THESE LINKS:

ge.tt/3vHN9ZE2

mediafire.com/folder/yx98a81upr4xg/tex

app.box.com/s/dljssixw236ye7lbhhwfq21hlvbswvkk

app.box.com/s/jhxvyrbd9u7i0ysbf310sg98k4m8uteb

EMAIL ANY COMMENTS TO DAVENPORTPRESS@GMAIL.COM .

APPENDIX B:
SAMPLE FILLED OUT LEGAL FORMS

The rest of this book has sample filled out legal forms including sample Wills.

All forms in this book can be filled out by pen or marker, or by using a computer. But people should be sure to handwrite signatures and nearby dates in permanent ink.

For forms with blank lines people can type or handwrite words into these however wanted, and can:

   1) type in (or handwrite) words into a line ("I appoint ___John Doe____ as Agent"),

   2) use underlining so added words look underlined, maybe using whited out commas to hold underlining ("I appoint __John Doe__ as Agent"), or

   3) remove blank lines so it looks like normal text ("I appoint John Doe as Agent"), but removing lines can make added words hard to see so some people put added words in bold ("I appoint **John Doe** as Agent").

SAMPLE FILLED OUT
FORM 1:
LAST WILL AND TESTAMENT (WITH GUARDIANS)

LAST WILL AND TESTAMENT

I, ___Henry James Ford___, a resident of __Travis__ County, , Texas, being of sound and disposing mind and memory, do hereby make, publish, and declare this as my Last Will and Testament (called here my "Will"), and hereby expressly revoke any Wills and Codicils earlier made by me.

1. GIFTS. I give the following gifts which are specific gifts except any gifts of money amounts are general gifts.

I give _antique oak tables and chairs_____
to _Anne Janet Lynn-Hutchinson_____ if they survive me.

I give __63 Ivy Road, Lundy, Texas, including land, buildings, and fixtures_____
to ___Greta Olivia Parupski_____ if they survive me.

I give _Bronze Roman Lamp_____
to _Anne Janet Lynn-Hutchinson_____ if they survive me.

I give ___1.5 carat diamond_____ to _Ruth Ann Jones_ if they survive me.

I give __$7,281.35_____ to _Wanda Kay Zinski_ if they survive me.

I give _Irish engraved ring____ to _Harriet Rush Smith_ if they survive me.

I give _all jewelry not given above_ to _Hannah Eve Pidoski_ if they survive me.

I give _UBank account ending #8923_ to _John Kent my cousin_ if they survive me.

I give _1998 Ford truck____ to _John Hatcher my cousin_ if they survive me.

I give _____
to _____ if they survive me.

2. TANGIBLE PERSONAL PROPERTY LISTS. I may leave signed lists or other writings giving tangible personal property, and although such writings may not be legally enforceable I request but do not require people follow such writings.

3. RESIDUE. I give the rest, residue, and remainder of my estate including all property I can distribute by Will not distributed by the preceding provisions of this Will, including any real property, personal property, or other property of any kind and wherever located, whether now owned or later acquired by me (called in this Will the "residue"), to:

<u>Mary Jennifer Ford my wife</u> if they survive me, but if they all do not survive me I give the just described property to

<u>Eric Jay Ford and Jill Sue Hart my children</u> or their lineal descendants per stirpes. Part of this residue section may be left unfilled or empty, and used parts should be given effect.

4. ADMINISTRATION. I name and appoint <u>Mary Jennifer Ford my wife</u> as executor of my Will and my estate.

5. GUARDIANS. If any of my children have not reached age 18 I name and appoint <u>Margaret Kim Windsor my sister</u> to be guardian over the person of such children. I also name and appoint <u>Margaret Kim Windsor</u> as guardian of the estate for such children and their estate and property, and also for any other persons under age 18 who receive or possess property and their estate and property.

6. MISCELLANEOUS. The following applies to this Will and generally.

I direct my estate and Will be administered in as informal a way as reasonably possible.

Any executor is appointed and shall serve as independent executor and independent administration may be used, and I direct no action shall be had in the county court in relation to the settlement of my estate other than the probating and recording of this Will and the return of the statutory inventory, appraisement, and list of claims of my estate.

Plural, singular, or gender meanings do not limit any Will part, such as use of "they".

Any executor or guardian of any type acting under this Will or otherwise shall serve without bond, surety, or other security including for performance of their duties.

Any executor shall be paid no compensation for their work or time spent as executor.

An executor shall sell a gift unless all beneficiaries getting it agree on its use or sale.

No unfilled Will part is a mistake, and all parts of this Will should be given effect.

The priority of Will gifts of the same type is based on the order they appear.

The words "give" and "gift" mean the same as devise, bequest, grant, legacy or similar.

The words "survive" or "surviving" in a gift or other place creates an absolute condition that must be met or a gift fails and anti-lapse laws or similar have no effect.

Any person or entity not surviving me by 60 days shall be deemed to not survive me.

For gifts to multiple beneficiaries a non-surviving beneficiary's share goes to other beneficiaries in proportion to shares they are taking, including for the residue or if a gift requires or mentions survival, but not if an alternate beneficiary is provided in the Will.

Any executor and guardian of any type is given as much power, authority, and discretion that may be given by law, including power to (with no liability for change in value) sell, lease, assign, mortgage, invest, operate, hold, exchange and transfer any way any property including of the estate, settle claims for or against the estate or others, do any tax action or filing, and have power of sale for real property, all with no need for inventory or filing or any act of a court or others.

Any executor has power to take any action involving an ancillary estate, give different kinds, portions or undivided interests in property to beneficiaries and assign value to all things, and do any distribution or division of my estate or property in cash or in kind.

If a gift including of household items goes to several beneficiaries the executor shall have sole discretion how to divide the gift, taking into account feelings of beneficiaries and myself.

Any executor may any time and in any amount pay debts of mine or my estate they in their sole and absolute discretion finds are valid, enforceable, timely, and fair, including of a last illness, for funeral and related things, and all with no filing or act of court or others.

If any property is distributable under this Will to a minor person, I authorize my executor or other party to make distribution to a custodian for the minor under the Uniform Transfers to Minors Act of Texas or any other state, with any person named in this Will as guardian of the estate as custodian but even if they are available my executor may nominate another person.

Any successor including of an executor or guardian of any type named in this Will shall have all powers, privileges, immunities and exemptions their predecessor had.

Not giving anything or more to my children and other family is intentional and not a mistake.

The residue includes lapsed or failed gifts, insurance paid to the estate, inheritances owed testator, and property testator had power of appointment or testamentary disposition over.

TESTATOR

IN WITNESS WHEREOF, I hereunto subscribe my name and declare, publish, and acknowledge this as my Last Will and Testament as Testator all in the presence of the witnesses signing below, this 15th day of ___January___, 20 15 .

Henry James Ford
Testator

WITNESSES

The foregoing instrument was signed, published, and declared by the above Testator in our presence as the Last Will and Testament of such Testator, and we undersigned the Witnesses sign our names hereunto as witnesses at the request and in the presence of the such Testator and in the presence of each other, on this 15th day of ___January___, 20 15 .

Amy Janet Windsor   ___87 Main Street, Pottsville, TX 78402___
Witness   Address
Brian Adam Smith   ___6328 Forest Lane, Norris, TX 78403___
Witness   Address

SAMPLE FILLED OUT
FORM 2:
LAST WILL AND TESTAMENT (NO GUARDIANS)

LAST WILL AND TESTAMENT

I, ___David Roger Widowonski___ , of ___Liberty___ County, Texas, being of sound and disposing mind and memory, do hereby make, publish, and declare this as my Last Will and Testament (called here my "Will"), and hereby expressly revoke any Wills and Codicils earlier made by me.

1. GIFTS. I give the following gifts which are specific gifts except any gifts of money amounts are general gifts.

I give ___a total of $50,000___ to ___Brian Oscar Peterson, Michael Paul Peterson, and Mary Rebecca Hart___ if they survive me.

I give ___a total of $6,000___ to ___Beth Tina Smith and Frank M. Smith___ if they survive me.

I give ___$5,000___ to ___Loretta Marsha Switt in the hope she will help her daughter Megan Kara Smith___ if they survive me.

I give ___$3,000___ to ___Loretta Marsha Switt___ if they survive me.

I give ___Wells Fargo savings account ending in #8923___ to ___Lawrence Deer___ if they survive me.

I give ___$1,000___ to ___American Red Cross charity___ if they survive me.

I give ___$5,000___ to ___Fishy Smith my fishing buddy___ if they survive me.

I give ___$2,000___ to ___Mary Nixon___ but is she does not survive me then to ___Karen Kay Paulson___ .

I give ___all cars and trucks I own at my death___ to ___Victor Perez my mechanic___ if they survive me.

I give ___$7,002.21___ to ___Brenda Mary Hill but if she fails to survive me then to her brother William Matthew Hill___ .

2. TANGIBLE PERSONAL PROPERTY LISTS. I may leave signed lists or other writings giving tangible personal property, and although such writings may not be legally enforceable I request but do not require people follow such writings.

3. RESIDUE. I give the rest, residue, and remainder of my estate including all property I can distribute by Will not distributed by the preceding provisions of this Will, including any real property, personal property, or other property of any kind and wherever located, whether now owned or later acquired by me (called in this Will the "residue"), to:

_____ if they survive me, but if they all do not survive me I give the just described property to

    20% to Hector Samuel Widowonski,

    30% to Kenneth Paul Widowonski, and

    50% to Mary Janet Maxwell

or their lineal descendants per stirpes. Part of this residue section may be left unfilled or empty, and used parts should be given effect.

4. ADMINISTRATION. I name and appoint   Hector Samuel Widowonski   as executor of my Will and my estate.

5. MISCELLANEOUS. The following applies to this Will and generally.

I direct my estate and Will be administered in as informal a way as reasonably possible.

Any executor is appointed and shall serve as independent executor and independent administration may be used, and I direct no action shall be had in the county court in relation to the settlement of my estate other than the probating and recording of this Will and the return of the statutory inventory, appraisement, and list of claims of my estate.

Plural, singular, or gender meanings do not limit any Will part, such as use of "they".

Any executor or guardian of any type acting under this Will or otherwise shall serve without bond, surety, or other security including for performance of their duties.

Any executor shall be paid no compensation for their work or time spent as executor.

An executor shall sell a gift unless all beneficiaries getting it agree on its use or sale.

No unfilled Will part is a mistake, and all parts of this Will should be given effect.

The priority of Will gifts of the same type is based on the order they appear.

The words "give" and "gift" mean the same as devise, bequest, grant, legacy or similar.

The words "survive" or "surviving" in a gift or other place creates an absolute condition that must be met or a gift fails and anti-lapse laws or similar have no effect.

Any person or entity not surviving me by 60 days shall be deemed to not survive me.

For gifts to multiple beneficiaries a non-surviving beneficiary's share goes to other beneficiaries in proportion to shares they are taking, including for the residue or if a gift requires or mentions survival, but not if an alternate beneficiary is provided in the Will.

Any executor and guardian of any type is given as much power, authority, and discretion that may be given by law, including power to (with no liability for change in value) sell, lease, assign, mortgage, invest, operate, hold, exchange and transfer any way any property including of the estate, settle claims for or against the estate or others, do any tax action or filing, and have power of sale for real property, all with no need for inventory or filing or any act of a court or others.

Any executor has power to take any action involving an ancillary estate, give different kinds, portions or undivided interests in property to beneficiaries and assign value to all things, and do any distribution or division of my estate or property in cash or in kind.

If a gift including of household items goes to several beneficiaries the executor shall have sole discretion how to divide the gift, taking into account feelings of beneficiaries and myself.

Any executor may any time and in any amount pay debts of mine or my estate they in their sole and absolute discretion finds are valid, enforceable, timely, and fair, including of a last illness, for funeral and related things, and all with no filing or act of court or others.

If any property is distributable under this Will to a minor person, I authorize my executor or other party to make distribution to a custodian for the minor under the Uniform Transfers to Minors Act of Texas or any other state, with any person named in this Will as guardian of the estate as custodian but even if they are available my executor may nominate another person.

Any successor including of an executor or guardian of any type named in this Will shall have all powers, privileges, immunities and exemptions their predecessor had.

Not giving anything or more to my children and other family is intentional and not a mistake.

Residue includes lapsed or failed gifts, insurance paid to the estate, inheritances owed testator, and property testator had power of appointment or testamentary disposition over.

TESTATOR

IN WITNESS WHEREOF, I hereunto subscribe my name and declare, publish, and acknowledge this as my Last Will and Testament as Testator all in the presence of the witnesses signing below, this 3rd day of ___March___, 20 15 .

David Roger Widowsonki
Testator

WITNESSES

The foregoing instrument was signed, published, and declared by the above Testator in our presence as the Last Will and Testament of such Testator, and we undersigned the Witnesses sign our names hereunto as witnesses at the request and in the presence of the such Testator and in the presence of each other, on this 3rd day of ___March___, 20 15 .

Michael Frank Bjerk   87 Main Street, Waco, TX 79421
Witness   Address

Brian Douglas Thorpe   927 Hubert Street, Abilene, TX 79232
Witness   Address

82

SAMPLE FILLED OUT
ADDITIONAL SECOND COPY OF
FORM 1:
LAST WILL AND TESTAMENT (WITH GUARDIANS)

LAST WILL AND TESTAMENT

I, <u>Paul Eric Windsor a/k/a Petey Windsor</u>, of <u>Travis</u> County, Texas, being of sound and disposing mind and memory, do hereby make, publish, and declare this as my Last Will and Testament (called here my "Will"), and hereby expressly revoke any Wills and Codicils earlier made by me.

1. GIFTS. I give the following gifts which are specific gifts except any gifts of money amounts are general gifts.

I give <u>$10,000</u> to <u>the United States Cancer Society</u> if they survive me.

I give <u>$5,000 in total</u> to <u>my cousin David Krupp's children</u> if they survive me.

I give <u>$6,000 in total</u> to <u>my cousin Carol Brown's children</u> if they survive me.

I give <u>$500 each</u> to <u>each of my grandchildren</u> if they survive me.

2. TANGIBLE PERSONAL PROPERTY LISTS. I may leave signed lists or other writings giving tangible personal property, and although such writings may not be legally enforceable I request but do not require people follow such writings.

3. RESIDUE. I give the rest, residue, and remainder of my estate including all property I can distribute by Will not distributed by the preceding provisions of this Will, including any real property, personal property, or other property of any kind and wherever located, whether now owned or later acquired by me (called in this Will the "residue"), to:
_____ if they survive me, but if they all do not survive me I give the just described property to
<u>   my children John Terry Windsor, Pamela Kay Smith, Martha Fiona Peterson, Greta Samantha Windsor-Somonis, Vernon Chester Windsor, and Mary Kay Windsor,</u>
<u>   and my loved cousin Beverly Hannah Carlson,</u>
<u>   and my great friend William Frank Sommenheim</u>
or their lineal descendants per stirpes. Part of this residue section may be left unfilled or empty, and used parts should be given effect.

4. ADMINISTRATION. I name and appoint ___my son John Terry Windsor___ as executor of my Will and my estate.

5. GUARDIANS. If any of my children have not reached age 18 I name and appoint ___my son John Terry Windsor___ to be guardian over the person of such children. I also name and appoint ___my son John Terry Windsor___ as guardian of the estate for such children and their estate and property, and also for any other persons under age 18 who receive or possess property and their estate and property.

6. MISCELLANEOUS. The following applies to this Will and generally.

I direct my estate and Will be administered in as informal a way as reasonably possible.

Any executor is appointed and shall serve as independent executor and independent administration may be used, and I direct no action shall be had in the county court in relation to the settlement of my estate other than the probating and recording of this Will and the return of the statutory inventory, appraisement, and list of claims of my estate.

Plural, singular, or gender meanings do not limit any Will part, such as use of "they".

Any executor or guardian of any type acting under this Will or otherwise shall serve without bond, surety, or other security including for performance of their duties.

Any executor shall be paid no compensation for their work or time spent as executor.

An executor shall sell a gift unless all beneficiaries getting it agree on its use or sale.

No unfilled Will part is a mistake, and all parts of this Will should be given effect.

The priority of Will gifts of the same type is based on the order they appear.

The words "give" and "gift" mean the same as devise, bequest, grant, legacy or similar.

The words "survive" or "surviving" in a gift or other place creates an absolute condition that must be met or a gift fails and anti-lapse laws or similar have no effect.

Any person or entity not surviving me by 60 days shall be deemed to not survive me.

For gifts to multiple beneficiaries a non-surviving beneficiary's share goes to other beneficiaries in proportion to shares they are taking, including for the residue or if a gift requires or mentions survival, but not if an alternate beneficiary is provided in the Will.

Any executor and guardian of any type is given as much power, authority, and discretion that may be given by law, including power to (with no liability for change in value) sell, lease, assign, mortgage, invest, operate, hold, exchange and transfer any way any property including of the estate, settle claims for or against the estate or others, do any tax action or filing, and have power of sale for real property, all with no need for inventory or filing or any act of a court or others.

Any executor has power to take any action involving an ancillary estate, give different kinds, portions or undivided interests in property to beneficiaries and assign value to all things, and do any distribution or division of my estate or property in cash or in kind.

If a gift including of household items goes to several beneficiaries the executor shall have sole discretion how to divide the gift, taking into account feelings of beneficiaries and myself.

Any executor may any time and in any amount pay debts of mine or my estate they in their sole and absolute discretion finds are valid, enforceable, timely, and fair, including of a last illness, for funeral and related things, and all with no filing or act of court or others.

If any property is distributable under this Will to a minor person, I authorize my executor or other party to make distribution to a custodian for the minor under the Uniform Transfers to Minors Act of Texas or any other state, with any person named in this Will as guardian of the estate as custodian but even if they are available my executor may nominate another person.

Any successor including of an executor or guardian of any type named in this Will shall have all powers, privileges, immunities and exemptions their predecessor had.

Not giving anything or more to my children and other family is intentional and not a mistake.

The residue includes lapsed or failed gifts, insurance paid to the estate, inheritances owed testator, and property testator had power of appointment or testamentary disposition over.

TESTATOR

IN WITNESS WHEREOF, I hereunto subscribe my name and declare, publish, and acknowledge this as my Last Will and Testament as Testator all in the presence of the witnesses signing below, this 2nd day of ___July___, 20 15 .

Paul Eric Windsor
Testator

WITNESSES

The foregoing instrument was signed, published, and declared by the above Testator in our presence as the Last Will and Testament of such Testator, and we undersigned the Witnesses sign our names hereunto as witnesses at the request and in the presence of the such Testator and in the presence of each other, on this 2nd day of ___July___, 20 15 .

| _Olivia Joy Pawlenty_ | 87 Hastings Avenue, El Paso, TX 70403 |
| Witness | Address |

| _Roy Felix Pawlenty_ | 87 Hastings Avenue, El Paso, TX 70403 |
| Witness | Address |

SAMPLE FILLED OUT
ADDITIONAL SECOND COPY OF
FORM 2:
LAST WILL AND TESTAMENT (NO GUARDIANS)

LAST WILL AND TESTAMENT

I, **Ruth May Kent** of **Orange** County, Texas,, being of sound and disposing mind and memory, do hereby make, publish, and declare this as my Last Will and Testament (called here my "Will"), and hereby expressly revoke any Wills and Codicils earlier made by me.

1. **GIFTS.** I give the following gifts which are specific gifts except any gifts of money amounts are general gifts.

I give a total of $100,000 to: 50% to Abraham Daniel Walker, 40% to Amy Ann Hope, and 10% to Jennifer Kim Beaufort if they survive me;

I give $900 and my cat Bob to Wanda Gina Sorenson if she survives me;

I give 1987 Ford Truck and any other vehicles I own of any type to Reginald William Porter my nephew if they survive me;

I give $20,000 to Greg Paul Best but if they fail to survive me then to his wife Mary Gertrude Best;

I give $990 to each of my first cousins if they survive me;

I give $5,000 to St. Mary Angelica of the Cross which was my old church in Allentown if they survive me;

I give $2,250 to St. Joseph's my church if they survive me;.

I give $300 to Timmy Hart my paperboy if they survive me;

I give $20,000 to Juanita Chuzappa my helper but if they fail to survive me then to Juanita's Chuzappa's children;

I give $10,000 to Marion Dexter my neighbor but if they fail to survive me then to her husband Arthur Dexter; and

I give $10,000 total to Janet Wilkins, Miranda Britom, Cindy Spagor, Diana Linda Craigtown, and Teresa Germann if they survive me.

2. **TANGIBLE PERSONAL PROPERTY LISTS.** I may leave signed lists or other writings giving tangible personal property, and although such writings may not be legally enforceable I request but do not require people follow such writings.

3. RESIDUE. I give the rest, residue, and remainder of my estate including all property I can distribute by Will not distributed by the preceding provisions of this Will, including any real property, personal property, or other property of any kind and wherever located, whether now owned or later acquired by me (called in this Will the "residue"), to:

Wanda Kim Dallas my daughter if they survive me, but if they all do not survive me then I give the just described property to

Jane Carol Yancy and Paul Alan Kent my cousins or their lineal descendants per stirpes.

Part of this residue section may be left unfilled or empty, and used parts should be given effect.

4. ADMINISTRATION. I name and appoint **Wanda Kim Dallas my daughter** as executor of my Will and my estate.

5. MISCELLANEOUS. The following applies to this Will and generally.

I direct my estate and Will be administered in as informal a way as reasonably possible.

Any executor is appointed and shall serve as independent executor and independent administration may be used, and I direct no action shall be had in the county court in relation to the settlement of my estate other than the probating and recording of this Will and the return of the statutory inventory, appraisement, and list of claims of my estate.

Plural, singular, or gender meanings do not limit any Will part, such as use of "they".

Any executor or guardian of any type acting under this Will or otherwise shall serve without bond, surety, or other security including for performance of their duties.

Any executor shall be paid no compensation for their work or time spent as executor.

An executor shall sell a gift unless all beneficiaries getting it agree on its use or sale.

No unfilled Will part is a mistake, and all parts of this Will should be given effect.

The priority of Will gifts of the same type is based on the order they appear.

The words "give" and "gift" mean the same as devise, bequest, grant, legacy or similar.

The words "survive" or "surviving" in a gift or other place creates an absolute condition that must be met or a gift fails and anti-lapse laws or similar have no effect.

Any person or entity not surviving me by 60 days shall be deemed to not survive me.

For gifts to multiple beneficiaries a non-surviving beneficiary's share goes to other beneficiaries in proportion to shares they are taking, including for the residue or if a gift requires or mentions survival, but not if an alternate beneficiary is provided in the Will.

Any executor and guardian of any type is given as much power, authority, and discretion that may be given by law, including power to (with no liability for change in value) sell, lease, assign, mortgage, invest, operate, hold, exchange and transfer any way any property including of the estate, settle claims for or against the estate or others, do any tax action or filing, and have power of sale for real property, all with no need for inventory or filing or any act of a court or others.

Any executor has power to take any action involving an ancillary estate, give different kinds, portions or undivided interests in property to beneficiaries and assign value to all things, and do any distribution or division of my estate or property in cash or in kind.

If a gift including of household items goes to several beneficiaries the executor shall have sole discretion how to divide the gift, taking into account feelings of beneficiaries and myself.

Any executor may any time and in any amount pay debts of mine or my estate they in their sole and absolute discretion finds are valid, enforceable, timely, and fair, including of a last illness, for funeral and related things, and all with no filing or act of court or others.

If any property is distributable under this Will to a minor person, I authorize my executor or other party to make distribution to a custodian for the minor under the Uniform Transfers to Minors Act of Texas or any other state, with any person named in this Will as guardian of the estate as custodian but even if they are available my executor may nominate another person.

Any successor including of an executor or guardian of any type named in this Will shall have all powers, privileges, immunities and exemptions their predecessor had.

Not giving anything or more to my children and other family is intentional and not a mistake.

Residue includes lapsed or failed gifts, insurance paid to the estate, inheritances owed testator, and property testator had power of appointment or testamentary disposition over.

TESTATOR

IN WITNESS WHEREOF, I hereunto subscribe my name and declare, publish, and acknowledge this as my Last Will and Testament as Testator all in the presence of the witnesses signing below, 21st day of March , 20 15 .

Ruth May Kent

Testator

WITNESSES

The foregoing instrument was signed, published, and declared by the above Testator in our presence as the Last Will and Testament of such Testator, and we undersigned the Witnesses sign our names hereunto as witnesses at the request and in the presence of the such Testator and in the presence of each other, on 21st day of March , 20 15 .

Susan Harriet Rogers   87 Badger Road, Carlisle, TX 71033
Witness   Address

Lucy Ann Pamway   892 Franklin Street, Harrisburg, TX 72019
Witness   Address

SAMPLE FILLED OUT
FORM 3:
SELF-PROVING AFFIDAVIT

SELF-PROVING AFFIDAVIT

THE STATE OF TEXAS

COUNTY OF __**Bexar**____

     BEFORE ME, the undersigned authority, on this day personally appeared __**Eunice Gladys Widowski**, **Charles John Coe**, and **Edgar Vernon Rogers**____, known to me to be the Testator and the witnesses, respectively, whose names are subscribed to the annexed or foregoing instrument in their respective capacities, and, all of said persons being by me duly sworn, the said __**Eunice Gladys Widowski**, Testator, declared to me and to the said witnesses in my presence that said instrument is his or her last Will and testament, and that he or she had willingly made and executed it as his or her free act and deed; and the said witnesses, each on his or her oath stated to me, in the presence and hearing of the said Testator, that the said Testator had declared to them that said instrument is his or her last Will and testament, and that he or she executed same as such and wanted each of them to sign it as a witness; and upon their oaths each witness stated further that they did sign the same as witnesses in the presence of the said Testator and at his or her request; that he or she was at that time eighteen years of age or over (or being under such age, was or had been lawfully married, or was then a member of the armed forces of the United States, or an auxiliary of the armed forces of the United States, or the United States Maritime Service) and was of sound mind; and that each of said witnesses was then at least fourteen years of age.

                               Eunice Gladys Widowski
                               Testator

                               Charles John Cunningham
                               Witness

                               Edgar Vernon Rogers
                               Witness

     Subscribed and sworn to before me by the said __Eunice Gladys Widowski__, testator, and by the said __Charles John Cunningham__ and __Edgar Vernon Rogers__, witnesses, this __8th__ day of __January__ A.D. __2015__.

(SEAL)   (Signed) __*Mary Beth Nottingham*__
                                Notary Public, State of Texas

SAMPLE FILLED OUT
FORM 4:
TANGIBLE PERSONAL PROPERTY LIST

TANGIBLE PERSONAL PROPERTY LIST

I request but do not require family and other people after my death follow the gifts of property I write below. I understand in this form only tangible personal property should be given, so not land or buildings, not money, and not investments or accounts without a tangible form. A gift written below has no effect if a named recipient does not survive me by 60 days or if a Will specifically gives the property.

PROPERTY ITEMS GIFTED	NAMES OF RECIPIENTS
1998 Ford Truck	Samantha Bell
1.3 carat diamond ring	Abigail Sue Reed
Italian silver jewelry	Samantha Bell
14 ft power boat and kayak with paddles	Luke Mark Wheeler
Parkhurst-style bench	Rebecca Stewart
glass table and its wood chairs	Rebecca Stewart
set of 18 silver candlesticks	Mary and Cindy Lott
my wedding dress and shoes	Mary Lott
chainsaw with serial no. 382937	Larry Kelly
chainsaw with serial no. 89930484421	Brian Kelly
antique lanterns and repair kits for them	Jason Brooks
oak lamp usually kept on porch	Susan Ditcher
all sewing machines and fabrics	Mary Kay Poppler
rocking chair bought in Oregon	Robert Schmidt
all fishing poles and fishing equipment	Elwood Blues
coin collection in 8 glass cases	Millard Filmore

DATE: __May 2, 2016__   SIGNED: *John William Filmore*

94

SAMPLE FILLED OUT
FORM 5:
CODICIL

CODICIL

I, __Jennifer Kay Polka_, of _Harris_ County, Texas, declare this to be a Codicil to my Will dated __January 2, 2014_.

FIRST: I hereby do revoke the part of my Will that reads as follows:

___I give $20,000 to Paul Jacob Farmer if they survive me.___

___I give my 1967 Corvette to Ned Baker.___

SECOND: I hereby do add the following part to my Will:

___I give $20,000 to Eve Susan Farmer if they survive me.___

___I give my 2012 Ford Truck to Ned Baker.___

THIRD: In all other respects I do confirm and republish the above-described Will.

TESTATOR

IN WITNESS WHEREOF, I hereunto subscribe my name and declare, publish, and acknowledge this as my Codicil all in the presence of the witnesses signing below, this _2nd_ day of __March__, 2015.

Jennifer Kay Polka
Testator

WITNESSES

The foregoing instrument was signed, published, and declared by the above Testator in our presence as the Codicil of such Testator, and we undersigned the Witnesses sign our names hereunto as witnesses at the request and in the presence of the such Testator and in the presence of each other, on this _2nd_ day of __March__, 2015.

Susan Vera Chomsky   88 Hunter Street, Galveston, TX 77028__
Witness   Address

Norman Paul Chomsky   88 Hunter Street, Galveston, TX 77028__
Witness   Address

SAMPLE FILLED OUT
FORM 6:
MEDICAL POWER OF ATTORNEY

DISCLOSURE STATEMENT

INFORMATION CONCERNING
THE MEDICAL POWER OF ATTORNEY

THIS IS AN IMPORTANT LEGAL DOCUMENT. BEFORE SIGNING THIS DOCUMENT, YOU SHOULD KNOW THESE IMPORTANT FACTS:

Except to the extent you state otherwise, this document gives the person you name as your agent the authority to make any and all health care decisions for you in accordance with your wishes, including your religious and moral beliefs, when you are no longer capable of making them yourself. Because "health care" means any treatment, service, or procedure to maintain, diagnose, or treat your physical or mental condition, your agent has the power to make a broad range of health care decisions for you. Your agent may consent, refuse to consent, or withdraw consent to medical treatment and may make decisions about withdrawing or withholding life-sustaining treatment. Your agent may not consent to voluntary inpatient mental health services, convulsive treatment, psychosurgery, or abortion. A physician must comply with your agent's instructions or allow you to be transferred to another physician.

Your agent's authority begins when your doctor certifies that you lack the competence to make health care decisions.

Your agent is obligated to follow your instructions when making decisions on your behalf. Unless you state otherwise, your agent has the same authority to make decisions about your health care as you would have had.

It is important that you discuss this document with your physician or other health care provider before you sign it to make sure that you understand the nature and range of decisions that may be made on your behalf. If you do not have a physician, you should talk with someone else who is knowledgeable about these issues and can answer your questions. You do not need a lawyer's assistance to complete this document, but if there is anything in this document that you do not understand, you should ask a lawyer to explain it to you.

The person you appoint as agent should be someone you know and trust. The person must be 18 years of age or older or a person under 18 years of age who has had the disabilities of minority removed. If you appoint your health or residential care provider (e.g., your physician or an employee of a home health agency, hospital, nursing home, or residential care home, other than a relative), that person has to choose between acting as your agent or as your health or residential care provider; the law does not permit a person to do both at the same time.

You should inform the person you appoint that you want the person to be your health care agent. You should discuss this document with your agent and your physician and give each a signed copy. You should indicate on the document itself the people and institutions who have signed copies. Your agent is not liable for health care decisions made in good faith on your behalf.

Even after you have signed this document, you have the right to make health care decisions for yourself as long as you are able to do so and treatment cannot be given to you or stopped over your objection. You have the right to revoke the authority granted to your agent by informing your agent or your health or residential care provider orally or in writing or by your execution of a subsequent medical power of attorney. Unless you state otherwise, your appointment of a spouse dissolves on divorce.

This document may not be changed or modified. If you want to make changes in the document, you must make an entirely new one.

You may wish to designate an alternate agent in the event that your agent is unwilling, unable, or ineligible to act as your agent. Any alternate agent you designate has the same authority to make health care decisions for you.

THIS POWER OF ATTORNEY IS NOT VALID UNLESS:
(1) YOU SIGN IT AND HAVE YOUR SIGNATURE ACKNOWLEDGED BEFORE A NOTARY PUBLIC; OR
(2) YOU SIGN IT IN THE PRESENCE OF TWO COMPETENT ADULT WITNESSES. THE FOLLOWING PERSONS MAY NOT ACT AS ONE OF THE WITNESSES:

(1) the person you have designated as your agent;

(2) a person related to you by blood or marriage;

(3) a person entitled to any part of your estate after your death under a will or codicil executed by you or by operation of law;

(4) your attending physician;

(5) an employee of your attending physician;

(6) an employee of a health care facility in which you are a patient if the employee is providing direct patient care to you or is an officer, director, partner, or business office employee of the health care facility or of any parent organization of the health care facility; or

(7) a person who, at the time this power of attorney is executed, has a claim against any part of your estate after your death.

ACKNOWLEDGMENT OF DISCLOSURE STATEMENT

By signing immediately below I agree and state I have received, read, and understood the contents of the above Disclosure Statement prior to executing the Medical Power Of Attorney in this document.

Signature   *Thomas Maxwell Smith*

MEDICAL POWER OF ATTORNEY
DESIGNATION OF HEALTH CARE AGENT

I, _____*Thomas Maxwell Smith*_____ (insert your name) appoint:

Name: _____*Helen Maria Smith*_____

Address: _____*927 Main Street, San Antonio, TX 78205*_____ Phone: _____*210-555-8122*_____

as my agent to make any and all health care decisions for me, except to the extent I state otherwise in this document. This medical power of attorney takes effect if I become unable to make my own health care decisions and this fact is certified in writing by my physician.

LIMITATIONS ON THE DECISION-MAKING AUTHORITY OF MY AGENT ARE AS FOLLOWS: _____

_____

_____

_____

_____

_____

DESIGNATION OF ALTERNATE AGENT.

(You are not required to designate an alternate agent but you may do so. An alternate agent may make the same health care decisions as the designated agent if the designated agent is unable or unwilling to act as your agent. If the agent designated is your spouse, the designation is automatically revoked by law if your marriage is dissolved.)

If the person designated as my agent is unable or unwilling to make health care decisions for me, I designate the following persons to serve as my agent to make health care decisions for me as authorized by this document, who serve in the following order:

A. First Alternate Agent

Name: _____*Chester Gregory Smith*_____

Address: _____*203 Grady Av., Lundy, TX 78205*_____

Phone: _____*210-555-1234*_____

B. Second Alternate Agent

Name: _____

Address: _____

Phone: _____

The original of this document is kept at:
_____*927 Main Street, San Antonio, TX 78205*_____

The following individuals or institutions have signed copies:

Name: _____*Helen Maria Smith*_____ Address: _____*927 Main Street, San Antonio, TX*_____

Name: _____*Dr. Sara Levy*_____ Address: _____*Memorial Hospital, San Antonio, TX*_____

DURATION.

I understand that this power of attorney exists indefinitely from the date I execute this document unless I establish a shorter time or revoke the power of attorney. If I am unable to make health care decisions for myself when this power of attorney expires, the authority I have granted my agent continues to exist until the time I become able to make health care decisions for myself.

(IF APPLICABLE) This power of attorney ends on the following date: _____

PRIOR DESIGNATIONS REVOKED.

I revoke any prior medical power of attorney.

ACKNOWLEDGMENT OF DISCLOSURE STATEMENT.

I have been provided with a disclosure statement explaining the effect of this document. I have read and understand that information contained in the disclosure statement.

(YOU MUST DATE AND SIGN THIS POWER OF ATTORNEY. YOU MAY SIGN IT AND HAVE YOU SIGNATURE ACKNOWLEDGED BEFORE A NOTARY PUBLIC OR YOU MAY SIGN IT IN THE PRESENCE OF TWO COMPETENT ADULT WITNESSES.)

SIGNATURE ACKNOWLEDGED BEFORE NOTARY

I sign my name to this medical power of attorney on __11th__ day of _____ _July, 2015_____ (month, year) at _____San Antonio, Texas_____ (City and State).

Thomas Maxwell Smith (Signature)   _Thomas Maxwell Smith__ (Print Name)

State of Texas

County of ____Bexar_____

This instrument was acknowledged before me on ____July 11, 2015_____ (date) by _____Thomas Maxwell Smith____ (name of person acknowledging).

_____Mary Beth Nottingham_____

NOTARY PUBLIC, State of Texas

Notary's printed name: ____Mary Beth Nottingham_____

My commission expires: _____November 1, 2023_____

OR

SIGNATURE IN PRESENCE OF TWO COMPETENT ADULT WITNESSES

I sign my name to this medical power of attorney on ___ day of _____ (month, year) at _____ (City and State).

_____ (Signature)   _____ (Print Name)

STATEMENT OF FIRST WITNESS.

I am not the person appointed as agent by this document. I am not related to the principal by blood or marriage. I would not be entitled to any portion of the principal's estate on the principal's death. I am not the attending physician of the principal or an employee of the attending physician. I have no claim against any portion of the principal's estate on the principal's death. Furthermore, if I am an employee of a health care facility in which the principal is a patient, I am not involved in providing direct patient care to the principal and am not an officer, director, partner, or business office employee of the health care facility or of any parent organization of the health care facility.

Signature:_____

Print Name:_____   Date:_____

Address:_____

SIGNATURE OF SECOND WITNESS.

Signature:_____

Print Name:_____   Date:_____

Address:_____

SAMPLE FILLED OUT
FORM 7:
DIRECTIVE TO PHYSICIANS AND FAMILY
OR SURROGATES (LIVING WILL)

DIRECTIVE TO PHYSICIANS
AND FAMILY OR SURROGATES

Instructions for completing this document:

This is an important legal document known as an Advance Directive. It is designed to help you communicate your wishes about medical treatment at some time in the future when you are unable to make your wishes known because of illness or injury. These wishes are usually based on personal values. In particular, you may want to consider what burdens or hardships of treatment you would be willing to accept for a particular amount of benefit obtained if you were seriously ill.

You are encouraged to discuss your values and wishes with your family or chosen spokesperson, as well as your physician. Your physician, other health care provider, or medical institution may provide you with various resources to assist you in completing your advance directive. Brief definitions are listed below and may aid you in your discussions and advance planning. Initial the treatment choices that best reflect your personal preferences. Provide a copy of your directive to your physician, usual hospital, and family or spokesperson. Consider a periodic review of this document. By periodic review, you can best assure that the directive reflects your preferences.

In addition to this advance directive, Texas law provides for two other types of directives that can be important during a serious illness. These are the Medical Power of Attorney and the Out-of-Hospital Do-Not-Resuscitate Order. You may wish to discuss these with your physician, family, hospital representative, or other advisers. You may also wish to complete a directive related to the donation of organs and tissues.

DIRECTIVE

I, __**Leo James Frankowski**__, recognize that the best health care is based upon a partnership of trust and communication with my physician. My physician and I will make health care decisions together as long as I am of sound mind and able to make my wishes known. If there comes a time that I am unable to make medical decisions about myself because of illness or injury, I direct that the following treatment preferences be honored:

If, in the judgment of my physician, I am suffering with a terminal condition from which I am expected to die within six months, even with available life-sustaining treatment provided in accordance with prevailing standards of medical care:

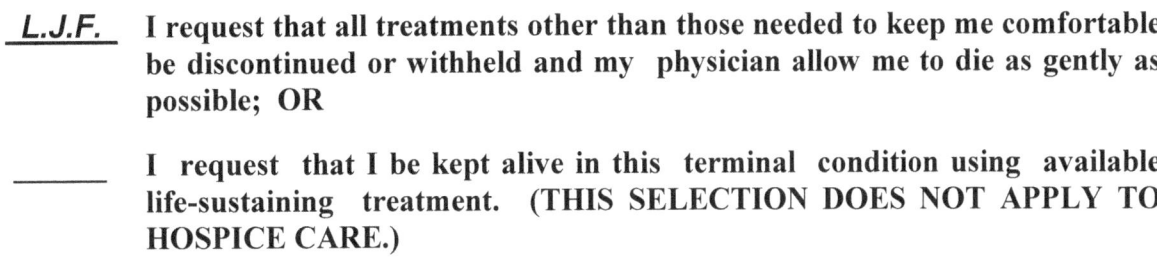

_L.J.F._   **I request that all treatments other than those needed to keep me comfortable be discontinued or withheld and my physician allow me to die as gently as possible; OR**

_____   **I request that I be kept alive in this terminal condition using available life-sustaining treatment. (THIS SELECTION DOES NOT APPLY TO HOSPICE CARE.)**

103

If, in the judgment of my physician, I am suffering with an irreversible condition so that I cannot care for myself or make decisions for myself and am expected to die without life-sustaining treatment provided in accordance with prevailing standards of care:

_L.J.F._   **I request that all treatments other than those needed to keep me comfortable be discontinued or withheld and my physician allow me to die as gently as possible; OR**

_____   **I request that I be kept alive in this irreversible condition using available life-sustaining treatment. (THIS SELECTION DOES NOT APPLY TO HOSPICE CARE.)**

Additional requests: (After discussion with your physician, you may wish to consider listing particular treatments in this space that you do or do not want in specific circumstances, such as artificial nutrition and fluids, intravenous antibiotics, etc. Be sure to state whether you do or do not want the particular treatment.)

_____

_____*None*_____

_____

_____

After signing this directive, if my representative or I elect hospice care, I understand and agree that only those treatments needed to keep me comfortable would be provided and I would not be given available life-sustaining treatments.

If I do not have a Medical Power of Attorney, and I am unable to make my wishes known, I designate the following person(s) to make treatment decisions with my physician compatible with my personal values:

    1._____ *see my Medical Power of Attorney* _____

    2._____

(If a Medical Power of Attorney has been executed, then an agent already has been named and you should not list additional names in this document.)

If the above persons are not available, or if I have not designated a spokesperson, I understand that a spokesperson will be chosen for me following standards specified in the laws of Texas. If, in the judgment of my physician, my death is imminent within minutes to hours, even with the use of all available medical treatment provided within the prevailing standard of care, I acknowledge that all treatments may be withheld or removed except those needed to maintain my comfort. I understand that under Texas law this directive has no effect if I have been diagnosed as pregnant. This directive will remain in effect until I revoke it. No other person may do so.

Signed   *Leo James Frankowski*   Date _____ *March 1, 2015* _____

City, County, State of Residence _____ *Austin, Travis County, Texas* _____

104

Two competent adult witnesses must sign below, acknowledging the signature of the declarant. The witness designated as Witness 1 may not be a person designated to make a treatment decision for the patient and may not be related to the patient by blood or marriage. This witness may not be entitled to any part of the estate and may not have a claim against the estate of the patient. This witness may not be the attending physician or an employee of the attending physician. If this witness is an employee of a health care facility in which the patient is being cared for, this witness may not be involved in providing direct patient care to the patient. This witness may not be an officer, director, partner, or business office employee of a health care facility in which the patient is being cared for or of any parent organization of the health care facility.

Witness 1 _*Jill Harriet Kulchek*_   Witness 2 _*Robert Harry King*_

Definitions:

"Artificial nutrition and hydration" means the provision of nutrients or fluids by a tube inserted in a vein, under the skin in the subcutaneous tissues, or in the stomach (gastrointestinal tract).

"Irreversible condition" means a condition, injury, or illness:
(1) that may be treated, but is never cured or eliminated;
(2) that leaves a person unable to care for or make decisions for the person's own self; and
(3) that, without life-sustaining treatment provided in accordance with the prevailing standard of medical care, is fatal.

Explanation: Many serious illnesses such as cancer, failure of major organs (kidney, heart, liver, or lung), and serious brain disease such as Alzheimer's dementia may be considered irreversible early on. There is no cure, but the patient may be kept alive for prolonged periods of time if the patient receives life-sustaining treatments. Late in the course of the same illness, the disease may be considered terminal when, even with treatment, the patient is expected to die. You may wish to consider which burdens of treatment you would be willing to accept in an effort to achieve a particular outcome. This is a very personal decision that you may wish to discuss with your physician, family, or other important persons in your life.

"Life-sustaining treatment" means treatment that, based on reasonable medical judgment, sustains the life of a patient and without which the patient will die. The term includes both life-sustaining medications and artificial life support such as mechanical breathing machines, kidney dialysis treatment, and artificial hydration and nutrition. The term does not include the administration of pain management medication, the performance of a medical procedure necessary to provide comfort care, or any other medical care provided to alleviate a patient's pain.

"Terminal condition" means an incurable condition caused by injury, disease, or illness that according to reasonable medical judgment will produce death within six months, even with available life-sustaining treatment provided in accordance with the prevailing standard of medical care.

Explanation: Many serious illnesses may be considered irreversible early in the course of the illness, but they may not be considered terminal until the disease is fairly advanced. In thinking about terminal illness and its treatment, you again may wish to consider the relative benefits and burdens of treatment and discuss your wishes with your physician, family, or other important persons in your life.

105

SAMPLE FILLED OUT
FORM 8:
DO-NOT-RESUSCITATE

OUT-OF-HOSPITAL DO-NOT-RESUSCITATE (OOH-DNR) ORDER
TEXAS DEPARTMENT OF STATE HEALTH SERVICES

 STOP DO NOT RESUSCITATE

This document becomes effective immediately on the date of execution for health care professionals acting in out-of-hospital settings. It remains in effect until the person is pronounced dead by authorized medical or legal authority or the document is revoked. Comfort care will be given as needed.

Person's full legal name __JOHN HARRISON SMITH__   Date of birth __6-22-1951__   ☒ Male ☐ Female

A. Declaration of the adult person: I am competent and at least 18 years of age. **I direct that none of the following resuscitation measures be initiated or continued for me:** cardiopulmonary resuscitation (CPR), transcutaneous cardiac pacing, defibrillation, advanced airway management, artificial ventilation.

Person's signature __JOHN HARRISON SMITH__   Date __11-19-2015__   Printed name __JOHN HARRISON SMITH__

B. Declaration by legal guardian, agent or proxy on behalf of the adult person who is incompetent or otherwise incapable of communication:

I am the: ☐ legal guardian;   ☐ agent in a Medical Power of Attorney; OR   ☐ proxy in a directive to physicians of the above-noted person who is incompetent or otherwise mentally or physically incapable of communication.

Based upon the known desires of the person, or a determination of the best interest of the person, **I direct that none of the following resuscitation measures be initiated or continued for the person: cardiopulmonary resuscitation (CPR), transcutaneous cardiac pacing, defibrillation, advanced airway management, artificial ventilation.**

Signature _____   Date _____   Printed name _____

C. Declaration by a qualified relative of the adult person who is incompetent or otherwise incapable of communication: I am the above-noted person's:

☐ spouse,   ☐ adult child,   ☐ parent, OR   ☐ nearest living relative, and I am qualified to make this treatment decision under Health and Safety Code §166.088.

To my knowledge the adult person is incompetent or otherwise mentally or physically incapable of communication and is without a legal guardian, agent or proxy. Based upon the known desires of the person or a determination of the best interests of the person, **I direct that none of the following resuscitation measures be initiated or continued for the person: cardiopulmonary resuscitation (CPR), transcutaneous cardiac pacing, defibrillation, advanced airway management, artificial ventilation.**

Signature _____   Date _____   Printed name _____

D. Declaration by physician based on directive to physicians by a person now incompetent or nonwritten communication to the physician by a competent person: I am the above-noted person's attending physician and have:

☐ seen evidence of his/her previously issued directive to physicians by the adult, now incompetent; OR   ☐ observed his/her issuance before two witnesses of an OOH-DNR in a nonwritten manner.

I direct that none of the following resuscitation measures be initiated or continued for the person: cardiopulmonary resuscitation (CPR), transcutaneous cardiac pacing, defibrillation, advanced airway management, artificial ventilation.

Attending physician's signature _____   Date _____   Printed name _____   Lic# _____

E. Declaration on behalf of the minor person: I am the minor's: ☐ parent;   ☐ legal guardian; OR   ☐ managing conservator.

A physician has diagnosed the minor as suffering from a terminal or irreversible condition. **I direct that none of the following resuscitation measures be initiated or continued for the person: cardiopulmonary resuscitation (CPR), transcutaneous cardiac pacing, defibrillation, advanced airway management, artificial ventilation.**

Signature _____   Date _____

Printed name _____

TWO WITNESSES: (See qualifications on backside.) We have witnessed the above-noted competent adult person or authorized declarant making his/her signature above and, if applicable, the above-noted adult person making an OOH-DNR by nonwritten communication to the attending physician.

Witness 1 signature __Samantha Maria Winchester__   Date __11-19-2015__   Printed name __Samantha Maria Winchester__

Witness 2 signature __Leroy Gregory Fields__   Date __11-19-2015__   Printed name __Leroy Gregory Fields__

Notary in the State of Texas and County of __Calhoun__. The above noted person personally appeared before me and signed the above noted declaration on this date: __11-19-2015__

Signature & seal: __Hector John Polk__   Notary's printed name: __Hector John Polk__   Notary Seal

[Note: Notary cannot acknowledge the witnessing of the person making an OOH-DNR order in a nonwritten manner]

PHYSICIAN'S STATEMENT: I am the attending physician of the above-noted person and have noted the existence of this order in the person's medical records. **I direct health care professionals acting in out-of-hospital settings, including a hospital emergency department, not to initiate or continue for the person: cardiopulmonary resuscitation (CPR), transcutaneous cardiac pacing, defibrillation, advanced airway management, artificial ventilation.**

Physician's signature __Dr. Helen Margaret Popchovski__   Date __11-19-2015__

Printed name __Dr. Helen Margaret Popchovski__   License # __12812947__

F. Directive by two physicians on behalf of the adult, who is incompetent or unable to communicate and without guardian, agent, proxy or relative: The person's specific wishes are unknown, but resuscitation measures are, in reasonable medical judgment, considered ineffective or are otherwise not in the best interests of the person. **I direct health care professionals acting in out-of-hospital settings, including a hospital emergency department, not to initiate or continue for the person: cardiopulmonary resuscitation (CPR), transcutaneous cardiac pacing, defibrillation, advanced airway management, artificial ventilation.**

Attending physician's signature _____   Date _____   Printed name _____   Lic# _____

Signature of second physician _____   Date _____   Printed name _____   Lic# _____

Physician's electronic or digital signature must meet criteria listed in Health and Safety Code §166.082(c).

All persons who have signed above must sign below, acknowledging that this document has been properly completed.

Person's signature __JOHN HARRISON SMITH__   Guardian/Agent/Proxy/Relative signature _____

Attending physician's signature __Dr. Helen Margaret Popchovski__   Second physician's signature _____

Witness 1 signature __Samantha Maria Winchester__   Witness 2 signature __Leroy Gregory Fields__   Notary's signature __Hector John Polk__

This document or a copy thereof must accompany the person during his/her medical transport.

INSTRUCTIONS FOR ISSUING AN OOH-DNR ORDER

PURPOSE: The Out-of-Hospital Do-Not-Resuscitate (OOH-DNR) Order on reverse side complies with Health and Safety Code (HSC), Chapter 166 for use by qualified persons or their authorized representatives to direct health care professionals to forgo resuscitation attempts and to permit the person to have a natural death with peace and dignity. This Order does NOT affect the provision of other emergency care, including comfort care.

APPLICABILITY: This OOH-DNR Order applies to health care professionals in out-of-hospital settings, including physicians' offices, hospital clinics and emergency departments.

IMPLEMENTATION: A competent adult person, at least 18 years of age, or the person's authorized representative or qualified relative may execute or issue an OOH-DNR Order. The person's attending physician will document existence of the Order in the person's permanent medical record. The OOH-DNR Order may be executed as follows:

Section A - If an adult person is competent and at least 18 years of age, he/she will sign and date the Order in Section A.

Section B - If an adult person is incompetent or otherwise mentally or physically incapable of communication and has either a legal guardian, agent in a medical power of attorney, or proxy in a directive to physicians, the guardian, agent, or proxy may execute the OOH-DNR Order by signing and dating it in Section B.

Section C - If the adult person is incompetent or otherwise mentally or physically incapable of communication and does not have a guardian, agent, or proxy, then a qualified relative may execute the OOH-DNR Order by signing and dating it in Section C.

Section D - If the person is incompetent and his/her attending physician has seen evidence of the person's previously issued proper directive to physicians or observed the person competently issue an OOH-DNR Order in a nonwritten manner, the physician may execute the Order on behalf of the person by signing and dating it in Section D.

Section E - If the person is a **minor** (less than 18 years of age), **who has been diagnosed by a physician as suffering from a terminal or irreversible condition,** then the minor's parents, legal guardian, or managing conservator may execute the OOH-DNR Order by signing and dating it in Section E.

Section F - If an adult person is incompetent or otherwise mentally or physically incapable of communication and does not have a guardian, agent, proxy, or available qualified relative to act on his/her behalf, then the attending physician may execute the OOH-DNR Order by signing and dating it in Section F with concurrence of a second physician (signing it in Section F) who is not involved in the treatment of the person or who is not a representative of the ethics or medical committee of the health care facility in which the person is a patient.

In addition, the OOH-DNR Order must be signed and dated by two competent adult witnesses, who have witnessed either the competent adult person making his/her signature in section A, or authorized declarant making his/her signature in either sections B, C, or E, and if applicable, have witnessed a competent adult person making an OOH-DNR Order by nonwritten communication to the attending physician, who must sign in Section D and also the physician's statement section. Optionally, a competent adult person or authorized declarant may sign the OOH-DNR Order in the presence of a notary public. However, a notary cannot acknowledge witnessing the issuance of an OOH-DNR in a nonwritten manner, which must be observed and only can be acknowledged by two qualified witnesses. Witness or notary signatures are not required when two physicians execute the OOH-DNR Order in section F. The original or a copy of a fully and properly completed OOH-DNR Order or the presence of an OOH-DNR device on a person is sufficient evidence of the existence of the original OOH-DNR Order and either one shall be honored by responding health care professionals.

REVOCATION: An OOH-DNR Order may be revoked at ANY time by the person, person's authorized representative, or physician who executed the order. Revocation can be by verbal communication to responding health care professionals, destruction of the OOH-DNR Order, or removal of all OOH-DNR identification devices from the person.

AUTOMATIC REVOCATION: An OOH-DNR Order is automatically revoked for a person known to be pregnant or in the case of unnatural or suspicious circumstances.

DEFINITIONS

Attending Physician: A physician, selected by or assigned to a person, with primary responsibility for the person's treatment and care and is licensed by the Texas Medical Board, or is properly credentialed and holds a commission in the uniformed services of the United States and is serving on active duty in this state. [HSC §166.002(12)].

Health Care Professional: Means physicians, nurses, physician assistants and emergency medical services personnel, and, unless the context requires otherwise, includes hospital emergency department personnel. [HSC §166.081(5)]

Qualified Relative: A person meeting requirements of HSC §166.088. It states that an adult relative may execute an OOH-DNR Order on behalf of an adult person who has not executed or issued an OOH-DNR Order and is incompetent or otherwise mentally or physically incapable of communication and is without a legal guardian, agent in a medical power of attorney, or proxy in a directive to physicians, and the relative is available from one of the categories in the following priority: 1) person's spouse; 2) person's reasonably available adult children; 3) the person's parents; or, 4) the person's nearest living relative. Such qualified relative may execute an OOH-DNR Order on such described person's behalf.

Qualified Witnesses: Both witnesses must be competent adults, who have witnessed the competent adult person making his/her signature in section A, or person's authorized representatives making his/her signature in either Sections B, C, or E on the OOH-DNR Order, or if applicable, have witnessed the competent adult person making an OOH-DNR by nonwritten communication to the attending physician, who signs in Section D. Optionally, a competent adult person, guardian, agent, proxy, or qualified relative may sign the OOH-DNR Order in the presence of a notary instead of two qualified witnesses. Witness or notary signatures are not required when two physicians execute the order by signing Section F. One of the witnesses must meet the qualifications in HSC §166.003(2), which requires that at least one of the witnesses not: (1) be designated by the person to make a treatment decision; (2) be related to the person by blood or marriage; (3) be entitled to any part of the person's estate after the person's death either under a will or by law; (4) have a claim at the time of the issuance of the OOH-DNR against any part of the person's estate after the person's death; or, (5) be the attending physician; (6) be an employee of the attending physician or (7) an employee of a health care facility in which the person is a patient if the employee is providing direct patient care to the patient or is an officer, director, partner, or business office employee of the health care facility or any parent organization of the health care facility.

Report problems with this form to the Texas Department of State Health Services (DSHS) or order OOH-DNR Order/forms or identification devices at (512) 834-6700.

Declarant's, Witness', Notary's, or Physician's electronic or digital signature must meet criteria outlined in HSC §166.011

Publications No. EF01-11421 - Revised July 1, 2009 by the Texas Department of State Health Services

SAMPLE FILLED OUT
FORM 9:
STATUTORY DURABLE POWER OF ATTORNEY

STATUTORY DURABLE POWER OF ATTORNEY

NOTICE: THE POWERS GRANTED BY THIS DOCUMENT ARE BROAD AND SWEEPING. THEY ARE EXPLAINED IN THE DURABLE POWER OF ATTORNEY ACT, SUBTITLE P, TITLE 2, ESTATES CODE. IF YOU HAVE ANY QUESTIONS ABOUT THESE POWERS, OBTAIN COMPETENT LEGAL ADVICE. THIS DOCUMENT DOES NOT AUTHORIZE ANYONE TO MAKE MEDICAL AND OTHER HEALTH-CARE DECISIONS FOR YOU. YOU MAY REVOKE THIS POWER OF ATTORNEY IF YOU LATER WISH TO DO SO.

You should select someone you trust to serve as your agent (attorney in fact). Unless you specify otherwise, generally the agent's (attorney in fact's) authority will continue until:

(1) you die or revoke the power of attorney;

(2) your agent (attorney in fact) resigns or is unable to act for you; or

(3) a guardian is appointed for your estate.

I, _Leo James Frankowski, 27 Main Street, Lee, TX_ (insert your name and address), appoint _Wanda Marie Frankowski, 27 Main Street, Lee, TX_ (insert the name and address of the person appointed) as my agent (attorney in fact) to act for me in any lawful way with respect to all of the following powers that I have initialed below.

TO GRANT ALL OF THE FOLLOWING POWERS, INITIAL THE LINE IN FRONT OF (N) AND IGNORE THE LINES IN FRONT OF THE OTHER POWERS LISTED IN (A) THROUGH (M).

TO GRANT A POWER, YOU MUST INITIAL THE LINE IN FRONT OF THE POWER YOU ARE GRANTING.

TO WITHHOLD A POWER, DO NOT INITIAL THE LINE IN FRONT OF THE POWER. YOU MAY, BUT DO NOT NEED TO, CROSS OUT EACH POWER WITHHELD.

_____ (A) Real property transactions;

_____ (B) Tangible personal property transactions;

_____ (C) Stock and bond transactions;

_____ (D) Commodity and option transactions;

_____ (E) Banking and other financial institution transactions;

_____ (F) Business operating transactions;

_____ (G) Insurance and annuity transactions;

_____ (H) Estate, trust, and other beneficiary transactions;

_____ (I) Claims and litigation;

_____ (J) Personal and family maintenance;

_____ (K) Benefits from social security, Medicare, Medicaid, or other governmental programs or civil or military service;

_____ (L) Retirement plan transactions;

_____ (M) Tax matters;

_L.J.F._ (N) ALL OF THE POWERS LISTED IN (A) THROUGH (M). YOU DO NOT HAVE TO INITIAL THE LINE IN FRONT OF ANY OTHER POWER IF YOU INITIAL LINE (N).

SPECIAL INSTRUCTIONS:

Special instructions applicable to gifts (initial in front of the following sentence to have it apply):

_____ I grant my agent (attorney in fact) the power to apply my property to make gifts outright to or for the benefit of a person, including by the exercise of a presently exercisable general power of appointment held by me, except that the amount of a gift to an individual may not exceed the amount of annual exclusions allowed from the federal gift tax for the calendar year of the gift.

ON THE FOLLOWING LINES YOU MAY GIVE SPECIAL INSTRUCTIONS LIMITING OR EXTENDING THE POWERS GRANTED TO YOUR AGENT.

_____

I trust my agent. I give power in this document so it is a general power of attorney and my agent shall have power and authority to perform or take any action I could do if I were personally present.

_____

_____

_____

_____

UNLESS YOU DIRECT OTHERWISE ABOVE, THIS POWER OF ATTORNEY IS EFFECTIVE IMMEDIATELY AND WILL CONTINUE UNTIL IT IS REVOKED. CHOOSE ONE OF THE FOLLOWING ALTERNATIVES BY CROSSING OUT THE ALTERNATIVE NOT CHOSEN:

(A) This power of attorney is not affected by my subsequent disability or incapacity.

(B) ~~This power of attorney becomes effective upon my disability or incapacity.~~

YOU SHOULD CHOOSE ALTERNATIVE (A) IF THIS POWER OF ATTORNEY IS TO BECOME EFFECTIVE ON THE DATE IT IS EXECUTED.

IF NEITHER (A) NOR (B) IS CROSSED OUT, IT WILL BE ASSUMED THAT YOU CHOSE ALTERNATIVE (A).

If Alternative (B) is chosen and a definition of my disability or incapacity is not contained in this power of attorney, I shall be considered disabled or incapacitated for purposes of this power of attorney if a physician certifies in writing at a date later than the date this power of attorney is executed that, based on the physician's medical examination of me, I am mentally incapable of managing my financial affairs. I authorize the physician who examines me for this purpose to disclose my physical or mental condition to another person for purposes of this power of attorney. A third party who accepts this power

111

of attorney is fully protected from any action taken under this power of attorney that is based on the determination made by a physician of my disability or incapacity.

I agree that any third party who receives a copy of this document may act under it. Revocation of the durable power of attorney is not effective as to a third party until the third party receives actual notice of the revocation. I agree to indemnify the third party for any claims that arise against the third party because of reliance on this power of attorney.

If any agent named by me dies, becomes legally disabled, resigns, or refuses to act, I name the following (each to act alone and successively, in the order named) as successor(s) to that
_____*Frances Marie Frankowski*_____ .

Signed this __*17th*__ day of __*December*__ , __*2014*__ .
_____*Leo James Frankowski*_____
(your signature)

State of __*Texas*__

County of __*Bexar*__

This document was acknowledged before me on ___*December 17, 2014*___ (date) by
_____*Leo James Frankowski*_____ (name of principal).

_____*Mary Beth Nottingham*_____
(signature of notarial officer)

(Seal, if any, of notary) _____
(printed name) ___*Mary Beth Nottingham*____
My commission expires: ____*November 1, 2023*____

IMPORTANT INFORMATION FOR AGENT (ATTORNEY IN FACT)

Agent's Duties

When you accept the authority granted under this power of attorney, you establish a "fiduciary" relationship with the principal. This is a special legal relationship that imposes on you legal duties that continue until you resign or the power of attorney is terminated or revoked by the principal or by operation of law. A fiduciary duty generally includes the duty to:

(1)   act in good faith;
(2)   do nothing beyond the authority granted in this power of attorney;
(3)   act loyally for the principal's benefit;

(4)   avoid conflicts that would impair your ability to act in the principal's best interest; and

(5)   disclose your identity as an agent or attorney in fact when you act for the principal by writing or printing the name of the principal and signing your own name as "agent" or "attorney in fact" in the following manner:

(Principal's Name) by (Your Signature) as Agent (or as Attorney in Fact)

In addition, the Durable Power of Attorney Act (Subtitle P, Title 2, Estates Code) requires you to:

(1)   maintain records of each action taken or decision made on behalf of the principal;

(2)   maintain all records until delivered to the principal, released by the principal, or discharged by a court; and

(3)   if requested by the principal, provide an accounting to the principal that, unless otherwise directed by the principal or otherwise provided in the Special Instructions, must include:

(A)   the property belonging to the principal that has come to your knowledge or into your possession;

(B)   each action taken or decision made by you as agent or attorney in fact;

(C)   a complete account of receipts, disbursements, and other actions of you as agent or attorney in fact that includes the source and nature of each receipt, disbursement, or action, with receipts of principal and income shown separately;

(D)   a listing of all property over which you have exercised control that includes an adequate description of each asset and the asset's current value, if known to you;

(E)   the cash balance on hand and the name and location of the depository at which the cash balance is kept;

(F)   each known liability;

(G)   any other information and facts known to you as necessary for a full and definite understanding of the exact condition of the property belonging to the principal; and

(H)   all documentation regarding the principal's property.

Termination of Agent's Authority

You must stop acting on behalf of the principal if you learn of any event that terminates this power of attorney or your authority under this power of attorney. An event that terminates this power of attorney or your authority to act under this power of attorney includes:

(1)   the principal's death;

(2)   the principal's revocation of this power of attorney or your authority;

(3)   the occurrence of a termination event stated in this power of attorney;

(4)   if you are married to the principal, the dissolution of your marriage by court decree of divorce or annulment;

(5)   the appointment and qualification of a permanent guardian of the principal's estate; or

(6)   if ordered by a court, the suspension of this power of attorney on the appointment and qualification of a temporary guardian until the date the term of the temporary guardian expires.

Liability of Agent

The authority granted to you under this power of attorney is specified in the Durable Power of Attorney Act (Subtitle P, Title 2, Estates Code). If you violate the Durable Power of Attorney Act or act beyond the authority granted, you may be liable for any damages caused by the violation or subject to prosecution for misapplication of property by a fiduciary under Chapter 32 of the Texas Penal Code.

THE ATTORNEY IN FACT OR AGENT, BY ACCEPTING OR ACTING UNDER THE APPOINTMENT, ASSUMES THE FIDUCIARY AND OTHER LEGAL RESPONSIBILITIES OF AN AGENT.

SAMPLE FILLED OUT
FORM 10:
AUTHORIZATION AGREEMENT FOR
NONPARENT RELATIVE (OVER CHILD)

AUTHORIZATION AGREEMENT FOR NONPARENT RELATIVE OR VOLUNTARY CAREGIVER

This authorization agreement is made in conformance with Chapter 34 of the Texas Family Code concerning the following Child:

Child's Full Name:	Noah Michael Smith
Date of Birth:	12-4-2011

Parent completing this form:

Full Name:	Mary Susan Smith
Physical Address:	88 Main Street, Galveston, TX 77555
Telephone Number:	281-555-4444
Other contact information:	

Child's other parent:

Full Name:	Kevin Michael Smith
Physical Address:	88 Main Street, Galveston, TX 77555
Telephone Number:	work phone 281-555-8877
Other contact information:	cell phone 281-555-1111

Parent voluntarily authorizes the following relative or Parental Child Safety Placement voluntary caregiver to make certain decisions regarding the child, as listed on the next page of this authorization agreement.

Name:	Evelyn Gladys Swanson
Relationship to Child (check one): Child's Grandparent ☒ Child's Adult Sibling ☐ Child's Aunt or Uncle ☐ Parental Child Safety Placement Voluntary Caregiver in accordance with Child Protective Services ☐	
Physical Address:	8977 Pine Forest Lane, Lundy, TX 77201
Telephone Number:	713-555-2222
Other contact information:	

PARENT AND RELATIVE OR VOLUNTARY CAREGIVER UNDERSTAND THAT THEY ARE REQUIRED BY LAW TO IMMEDIATELY PROVIDE EACH OTHER WITH INFORMATION REGARDING ANY CHANGE IN THE OTHER PARTY'S ADDRESS OR CONTACT INFORMATION.

Parent authorizes the above named relative or voluntary caregiver to perform the following acts in regard to the child and the relative or voluntary caregiver assumes the responsibility of performing these functions:

(1) To authorize medical, dental, psychological, surgical treatment, and immunization of the child, including executing any consents or authorizations for the release of information as required by law relating to the treatment or immunization;

(2) To obtain and maintain health insurance coverage for the child and automobile insurance coverage for the child, if appropriate;

(3) To enroll the child in a day-care program or public or private preschool, primary or secondary school;

(4) To authorize the child to participate in age-appropriate extracurricular, civic, social, or recreational activities, including athletic activities;

(5) To authorize the child to obtain a learner's permit, driver's license, or state-issued identification card;

(6) To authorize employment of the child; and

(7) To apply for and receive public benefits on behalf of the child.

(8) This authorization agreement does not confer on the relative or voluntary caregiver of the child the right to authorize the performance of an abortion on the child or the administration of emergency contraception to the child

To the best of the parent's and the relative's or voluntary caregiver's knowledge (check if applicable):

☒ This child is not the subject of a current (pre-existing) valid authorization agreement, and no parent, guardian, custodian, licensed child-placing agency or other agency makes any claim to actual physical possession or care, custody or control of the child that is inconsistent with this authorization agreement.

To the best of the parent's and the relative's or voluntary caregiver's knowledge (choose one from below):

☒ THERE IS NO COURT INVOLVEMENT WITH THIS CHILD
All of the following statements must apply:
- There is no court order or pending suit affecting the parent-child relationship concerning the child.
- There is no pending litigation in any court concerning custody, possession, or placement of the child or access to or visitation with the child.
- The court does not have continuing jurisdiction concerning the child.

☐ THIS CHILD HAS BEEN THE SUBJECT OF A COURT ACTION
The court with continuing jurisdiction concerning the child has given written approval for the execution of the authorization agreement accompanied by the following information:
- The county in which the court is located;
- The number of the court; and
- The cause number in which the order was issued or the litigation is pending.
Please staple a copy of the court's order to this agreement.

WARNINGS AND DISCLOSURES

This authorization agreement is an important legal document. The parent and the relative or voluntary caregiver must read all of the warnings and disclosures before signing this authorization agreement.

The parent and relative are not required to consult an attorney but are advised to do so.

A parent's rights as a parent may be adversely affected by placing or leaving the parent's child with another person.

This authorization agreement does not confer on the relative or voluntary caregiver the rights of a managing or possessory conservator or legal guardian.

A parent who is a party to this authorization agreement may terminate the authorization agreement and resume custody, possession, care, and control of the child on demand and at any time the parent may request the return of the child.

Failure by the relative or voluntary caregiver to return the child to the parent immediately on request may have criminal and civil consequences.

Under other applicable law, the relative or voluntary caregiver may be liable for certain expenses relating to the child in the relative's or voluntary caregiver's care, but the parent still retains the parental obligation to support the child.

In certain circumstances, this authorization agreement may not be entered into without written permission of the court. Examples of when court permission must be granted include when a court has entered a previous order granting custody or establishing a child support obligation.

This authorization agreement may be terminated by certain court orders affecting the child.

This authorization agreement does not supersede, invalidate, or terminate any prior authorization agreement regarding the child.

This authorization agreement is void if a prior authorization agreement regarding the child is in effect and has not expired or been terminated.

MAILING REQUIREMENTS:
When both parents do not sign the parent authorization agreement, a copy of the agreement MUST be mailed to the non-signing parent, unless that parent is deceased or has had his or her parental rights terminated. This authorization agreement **is void** unless:
1. The parties mail a copy of this agreement to a non-signing parent **not later than the 10th day** after the date the authorization agreement is signed, **by certified or international registered mail**, as applicable, *return receipt requested*.
2. If the parties do not receive a response from the non-signing parent before the 20th day after the date the copy of the agreement is mailed, the parties must mail a second copy of the agreement **by first class mail or international first class mail**, as applicable, to the parent **not later than the 45th day** after the date the authorization agreement is signed.

EXCEPTION TO MAILING REQUIREMENTS:
If a parent who did not sign the authorization agreement **does not have court-ordered possession of or access to the child who is the subject of the agreement**, the parent who is a party to the agreement does not have to mail a copy of the agreement to the non-signing parent if either of the following circumstances applies:
1. A protective order has been issued against the non-signing parent as provided under Chapter 85 of the Texas Family Code or under a similar law of another state for committing an act of family violence (as defined by Section 71.004 of the Texas Family Code) against the parent

who signed the agreement or any child of the parent who signed the agreement; or

2. The non-signing parent has been convicted of any of the following criminal offenses against the parent who signed the agreement or any child of the parent who signed the agreement:

   o any offense under Title 5 of the Texas Penal Code (including murder, homicide, kidnapping, assault and sexual assault); or

   o any other criminal offense in Texas or any other state if the offense involves a violent act or prohibited sexual conduct.

This authorization agreement (select one of the following two):

☐ Expires on this date: _____ OR

☒ Is valid until revoked in writing by either party

In addition, check here if you want the agreement to continue in effect after your death or during any period of incapacity. ☒

Execution of a subsequent authorization agreement does not by itself supersede, invalidate, or terminate a prior authorization agreement.

By signing below, parent and the relative or voluntary caregiver acknowledge that they have each read this authorization agreement carefully, are entering into the authorization agreement voluntarily, and have read and understand all of the Warnings and Disclosures included in this authorization agreement.

Mary Susan Smith
_____

PARENT
Printed name: Mary Susan Smith

SUBSCRIBED AND ACKNOWLEDGED BEFORE ME on this 7th day of December, 20 14.

Nathanial Peter Notario
_____
Notary Public in and for the State of TEXAS

Kevin Michael Smith
_____

PARENT**
Printed name: Kevin Michael Smith

SUBSCRIBED AND ACKNOWLEDGED BEFORE ME on this 7th day of December, 20 14.

Nathanial Peter Notario
_____
Notary Public in and for the State of TEXAS

Evelyn Gladys Swanson
_____

RELATIVE OR VOLUNTARY CAREGIVER
Printed name: Evelyn Gladys Swanson

SUBSCRIBED AND ACKNOWLEDGED BEFORE ME on this 9th day of December, 20 14.

Pam Judy Lott-Walker
_____
Notary Public in and for the State of TEXAS

SAMPLE FILLED OUT
FORM 11:
APPOINTMENT OF AGENT
TO CONTROL DISPOSITION OF REMAINS

APPOINTMENT OF AGENT TO
CONTROL DISPOSITION OF REMAINS

I, __John Brian Winchester, 83 Harrisburg Avenue, Houston, TX 77020__ ,
(your name and address)
being of sound mind, willfully and voluntarily make known my desire that, upon my
death, the disposition of my remains shall be controlled by __Charlie Paul Swanson__
(name of agent)
in accordance with Section 711.002 of the Health and Safety Code and, with respect to
that subject only, I hereby appoint such person as my agent (attorney-in-fact).

All decisions made by my agent with respect to the disposition of my remains, including
cremation, shall be binding.

SPECIAL DIRECTIONS: Set forth below are any special directions limiting the
power granted to my agent:

__I would like to have a simple church ceremony at St. Matt's but do not want anything__
__else, and I would like a white marble small tombstone like my brother Kent's__

AGENT:
Name: __Charlie Paul Swanson__
Address: __808 Buffalo Speedway, Bellaire, TX 77001__
Telephone Number: __713-555-0283__
Acceptance of Appointment: __*Charlie Paul Swanson*__
(signature of agent)
Date of Signature: __November 25, 2014__

SUCCESSORS: If my agent dies, becomes legally disabled, resigns, or refuses to act, I
hereby appoint the following persons (each to act alone and successively, in the order
named) to serve as my agent (attorney-in-fact) to control the disposition of my remains as
authorized by this document:

1. First Successor
Name: _____
Address: _____
Telephone Number: _____
Acceptance of Appointment: _____
(signature of first successor)

Date of Signature: _____

2. Second Successor

Name: _____

Address: _____

Telephone Number: _____

Acceptance of Appointment: _____
                                    (signature of second successor)

Date of Signature: _____

DURATION: This appointment becomes effective upon my death.

PRIOR APPOINTMENTS REVOKED: I hereby revoke any prior appointment of any person to control the disposition of my remains.

RELIANCE: I hereby agree that any cemetery organization, business operating a crematory or columbarium or both, funeral director or embalmer, or funeral establishment who receives a copy of this document may act under it. Any modification or revocation of this document is not effective as to any such party until that party receives actual notice of the modification or revocation. No such party shall be liable because of reliance on a copy of this document.

ASSUMPTION: THE AGENT, AND EACH SUCCESSOR AGENT, BY ACCEPTING THIS APPOINTMENT, ASSUMES THE OBLIGATIONS PROVIDED IN, AND IS BOUND BY THE PROVISIONS OF, SECTION 711.002 OF THE HEALTH AND SAFETY CODE.

Signed this __25th_ day of __November_____ , 20_14_ .

                              __*John Brian Winchester*___
                                    (your signature)

State of __Texas___
County of __Harris_____
   This document was acknowledged before me on __Nov. 25, 2014___ (date) by
   _John Brian Winchester____ (name of principal).

__*Nathan Eric Notariolo*____
   signature of notarial officer
      (seal, if any, of notary) _____
      (printed name) __Nathan Eric Notariolo___
      My commission expires: __Jan. 1, 2020___

ABOUT THE BOOK AUTHOR

MANFRED STERNBERG, TEXAS LAWYER

Manfred Sternberg received his law degree from Louisiana State University in 1985 and has been practicing law in Houston, Texas for almost 30 years. His work includes Wills, trusts, estate planning, tax, health care law, family law, real estate law, business law, loans and financing, and Texas gaming law.

In 1993 Manfred was one of the first Texas lawyers to be Board Certified in Consumer and Commercial Law by the Texas Board of Legal Specialization. He has a special interest in helping medical patients and consumers and was named Texas Health Services Authority chairman by Governor Rick Perry. Manfred has served in several other state positions trying to protect people and make the law work for them.

Manfred is an experienced business lawyer and has helped hundreds of businesses over 30 years including Citicorp, Bank of America, Shell Western E&P, Transamerica Insurance, and the Houston Rockets basketball team. He has been chief corporate counsel in charge of legal matters for several successful businesses. Manfred himself has founded, owned, and operated a variety of businesses including Zebec Data, Citadel Computer, Commercial Capital Trading, and Bluegate Corporation.

Manfred wrote the book and course "How To Buy Real Estate With Crowdfunding" on buying real estate with a crowd of people who want to invest big or small amounts. He also wrote the book "Davenport's Louisiana Wills And Estate Planning Legal Forms".

Manfred is married with 2 children and lives in Houston, Texas

Manfred and other lawyers at his Texas law firm are available to help people with Wills, estate planning, tax issues, health care forms, and other matters.

CONTACT INFORMATION

MANFRED STERNBERG & ASSOCIATES PC

4550 Post Oak Pl. Dr., Suite 119, Houston, TX 77027

manfred@manfredlaw.com   713-622-4300